THIS AGE LIVES AND LEFTS!!

LET LIFE LIVE

SIKANDA

Contents

Hey ! Energetic and excited yet stressed and confused teenagers .

How is this age going ?

I think , my experience and my poems can help you have a clear heart and mind .

And I also hope that you will find understanding and relatability in my work.

Chapters : Life from different shades

ONE

THE ALMIGHTY

… main iski kaynaat ka ek fanka hun phir bhi , Khuda mujhe asmaan ki zameen jitni ehmiyat deta hh .

kisi insaan ki tarah meri choti choti khushiyan ka khayal rakhta hh

Aulad ki tarah meri saari shikayatein or zarooratein sunta hh

meri takleefon ki khabar rahkhta hh

oor chupke se kisi hawa ki tarah dil mein utarkar meri dawa banta hh …

From a girl who often said to her mom ," Mummy! vrat mat rakha karo , bhagwan naam ki koi cheez nahin hoti, GOD is an illogical myth and science and logic is that what is running this world to a girl who only trusts HIM , who feels only HIS presence in whatever happens in her life and who justifies all her pains just in her faith.

It took nineteen years for me to connect with him ,to find him in the melancholy air of my life ,to literally discover his existence and things started changing for me … I felt heard, I felt healed, I felt being understood after years of breathing in a body which was complaining ,over expecting ,kind undeserving, impatient, immature and stubborn.

The Real me identified with my soul after I tried to identify with HIM . He gave me all that I needed to survive in this community of oversmart people ,materialistic ,egoistic and hypocrite souls . I daily feel as if he pats on my back to tell me - Go for this day, I am there as if he says M Sambhal Lunga, tu chal toh sahi!! In short , he completed my life with him, now I am all HIS.

Its not like I never had problems or pains or unanswered questions or like my hope didn't allow me to cry, complain ,be sad and feel helpless . I have also had terrible and tragic experiences like everyone else whose life had a fate and some of its factors remaining uncontrolled throughout the journey of life. I have also been face to face with shallowness, with uncertainties and suspenses which the immediacy unleashed on me and I was not mature enough (infact, even now I am not that mature) to let that GO or let just pass on not thinking this is just few moments ,not experienced enough about the tactics of fate and then I used to blame GOD like had he wanted this or that would have never happened and now ,my way has changed . I pass the burden of my tears on him and then it seems like HE fight my fights my fate.

He kept me alive when I wished death

He kept me awake when he thought I'd have a nightmare

He gifted me sleep after casting a beautiful dream

He gave me rational thoughts when I was overthinking stupid things

He enlightened me with intentions that everyone hid through my anxiety

He scolded me when I troubled myself too much through a headache

He snatched from me the empty book and handed a beautiful ink to scribble on the book he made in my heart, he reassured me everytime I cried my pains out by making me feel light ,he relieved me of the pressure to live this life a certain way and changed and beautified the colourful skies and many such innumerable, unrecognized efforts made by him while I strive to survive .

No doubt ,he knows everything but even He can't change things for us in a second .Its not like he will wash your life and then brighten it, make it ONLY filled with smile, purity, happiness, truthness like plains but you know what? No one would realise the significance of plains until one sees other creations on soil-like rugged mountains ,deep valleys unfertile though very holistic plateaus, running rivers and stagnant though alive oceans .These creations don't make the soil disturbed but the beauty of earth distributed in several forms and plains is just one of them .We spend our entire life searching for stability and trying to arrange things our way and make those things adjust which are inevitable.

- Maana ye uski apni kaynaat hh par iss kaynat k apne kuch usool hain

khuda ko vo saare kabool hain !!

There are some laws of life and problems are one of them .We can't be safe and isolated .Faith is just a option but it is the greatest force behind further choices .Trusting GOD ,to some people is like getting blind to everything and just praying but to me it is like having a farther vision like having the ability to look beyond the current situation. His name ,His feel ,His thoughts diffuse a power which makes the survival of physically blind and other differently abled people possible ;makes the identity of mentally triggered ,incompatible minds usually judged by everyone elevated ;makes sensitive people respect themselves .

Ankhein band karne ki ehmiyat tab samajh m aati h jab toofan tabah karne k irade lekar zindagi ki sarhad tak aata h

Jab har pal koi faisla lena hota hh jiska anjaam tak parakh paane ka waqt nahin milta ,tab dil ko Dua ki karamat ka pata chalta hh

Jab saari duniya apne apne fayde k liye saara dil tod deti h tab tukde ikathhe karne k liye honsle ki zaroorat ka pata chalta hh

Kayi baar insaan ki galti nahin hoti or Khuda ye janta hh ... bohot waqt lagta hh Khuda ko tumhe saza or imtehaan ka farq samjhane m .Khuda ki lagayi hui marham aahista kaam karti h par gam ko sabak k makaam tak le Jaa Kar jadd se saara dard khatam kar deti hh .Khuda vo taqat hh jiske asar ko azmaana bevakoofi h ,isse azmaya nahin sirf mehsoos Kiya jaata hh ,jiske ikhtiyaar mein zameen or asmaan donon hain phir bhi falak se tumhari duaon k badle apne naam mein farishte khak tak pohochata hh or jiski na koi hadd h na koi kamzori phir bhhi tumhari zindagiyon k maslon mein hi mashroof rehta hh . Khuda tumhe sabr sikhata hh par ek ek zulm ka badla tumhari oor se vo khud leta hh .

Sabse pukhta insaaf Khuda ki adalat mein hota hh

jisme na gawaah ki zaroorat or na saboot ki peshkash hoti hh sidha jo galat hh uski saza ka elaan hota hh .

Agar tum neki par ho ,paakdil ho ,taleem k dikhaye rasste par muntazir ho toh kisi se khofzada nahin hona...vo tumhari hifazat karega ... izzat karo har insaan ki par darro sirf usse jiske ek ishare par tumhari zindagi m qayamat aa sakti hh... vo sirf Khuda hh!

Uspe yakeen rakho ,tum nahin jante tumhare liye kitni cheezen vo abhi theek karne mein laga hua hh ,tumhare kal k liye tumhe tayyar karne mein laga hua hh ,tumhare liye vo sab jeet raha h jiske tum layak ho ...waqt anne par tumhe ye tohfe toh mil jayenge par jisne tumhari duaen sunke ,taqdeer tumhare haqq m ki hh ,ye saare ehtimaam kiye hain ;uske nishaan tumhe sirf hawayon m nazar aayenge .

Haa lagta h kabhi kabhi ki tamaam duniya ki mushkilat ,badquismati or benoor raatein usne tumhari zindagi mein likhdi ,ki ye saasien sirf bojh hain ,ki jo Khuda baaki sab pe meharbaan hh vo tumhe unsuna kar raha hh ...or ye sirf naumeedi ki jhalak hh koi gunnah nahin .Kuch haalat hamari sochne, sunne or samajhne ki taqat ko masoor bana dete hain ,ujaala nazar hi nahin aata ,hazaron koshisho k baad bhi nateeja hamare haqq mein nahin hota! Insaan tab bikhar jaata hh or bikhri hui rooh sirf cheenk sakti hh ,duaon mein vo narmi kaha se laye.

Par ye waqt kuch waqt baad unn panno sa ho jayega jo tumhare haalaton ne likhe...tabah toh nahin kar paoge unn panno ko lekin ...Khuda tumhe itni barkat bakshega ki aane wale panne tumhare likhe lafzon se chamak rahe honge.

Vo tab bhhi tumhara saath deta hh jab tum sikhayaton m aakar uska hath chatak dete ho kyuki vo waqif rehta hh tumhare banjar dil se or issliye vo jannat ki nadiyon ka rukh tumhari zimdagi ki orr kar raha hota hh .

Vo har manzar pe tumhare saath hh ...jab tum shuruaat karo ,jab ladkhadao ,jab giro phir utho ,jab thakk jao ,jab haar maan jao or tab bhhi jab koi manzil haasil karlo ... par usse pata hh kab tumhara kitna or kaise saath dena hh...kab tumhe dhakka dena hh...kab tumhe khud duniya se ladne dena hh .

Vo janta hh tumhari kabiliyat bhhi tumhari kamiya bhhintumhare kasoor bhhi issliye tum tumhe qabiliyat pesh karne ka moka deta hh ,tumhari kamiyo ko maaf kar deta hh or kasoor mutabik kaynat se sulook karwata hh !!

Agar kabhi duniya se bhagna chaho ,chhipna chaho ya unjaanon ki bheed m unjaan banna chaho toh tumhare liye raste bhi vo khojega or panaah bhhi or tumhara pata sirf usse pata hoga tumhe toh khabar bhi nahin hogi ki kudrat ki lakeerien tumhari band ankhon or bezabaan dil ko kaha lekar jaa rhi hain ... tum bas pohoch jaoge or kho jaoge khud mein kamaskam tab tak dil ke alfaaz tumhe dhundh na len ... tum naye ujalon mein nayi syahi m kisi khoobsurat kaagaz par Badi si duniya se vajood ki orr se nayi zindagi bayaan karoge or jab duniya k uss tukde m akele bass jaoge ,tum Khuda ko apni guftagu se khuda ki ehmiyat bata rahe hoge ... shukraguzar banoge ...Khuda ko apni wafadari ka wada de rahe hoge or Khuda tumse durson k liye insaaniyat or tumhare liye ek zinda dil maang raha hoga ...Haa har raaste to khoobsurat manzil hasil nahin hoti par Khuda har manzil k liye khoobsurat dil Bana deta h!

My words to GOD :
    Mujhe nahin pata tu kaha hh
    Par teri mutthi m taqdeer -e- jahan hh
    Tu sokhta h sabke gham jahan umeed dikhe tu vahan hh
    Jo manle uski zaban pe nahin toh Allah tu na manne walon ki bhi sun raha hh
    Kya kahu teri mojudgi k bare m ,har guzarte pal k saath tu apni hajari de raha hh
    M nahin janti tu kya hh ,agar sab kuch nahin toh sab m toh hh
    Tu na ho toh ankhein khuli or band hone ka farq bhi pata na chale varna band ankhon mein bhi. rang dikhayi den tu yahi toh hh
    Jo zindagi k safar se thakk gye hain ,tera zikr aane k baad kahen tune hamen zinda rakha tu sahi. toh hh
    Kuch logon se teri mehar ki mehak aati hh or vo mujhse puchte hain - tu thik toh hh ??

ᐅᐅᐅ

" Ae khuda, tune mujhe khuddari sikhayi ,khudgarzi k liye nahi
    Himmat bakshi bagavat k liye nahi
    Haqq ki baat batayi, haqq ki ana k liye nahi
    Har farq samjhaya ,har farq mitaya
    Har farz ko tohfa banaya ,har fasle ko mitane ka moka banaya
    Khwaishon ki azaadi bhi di or zimmedariyon ki bandagi bhi
    Sapne dekhne k liye ankhein bhi di or sabki sunne k liye kaan bhi
    Naseeb bhi diya naseeb se ladne ki ijazat bhi ...phir haar kyu tay ki
    Zindagi bhi di or har ehsaas ki hifazat bhi "

ᐅᐅᐅ

"Banda khwab , khwaish or khushiyan mangta hh

Or Khuda Imtehaan ,sabr or aitbar mangta hh"

ᗡᗡᗡ

"Log chahte hain unki umar khushiyon jitni hi ho
      Umar dene wale ko kon yaad rakhe agar aisa ho "

ᗡᗡᗡ

"Kisi ko bhi sab kuch nahi milta
      Par aisa koi nahi jisse kuch bhi nahi milta"
      Haa, lagta h kabhi kabhi chin gaya kuch bohot azeez
      Lagta h kabhi kabhi mil gaya kuch aisa jiske m kabil nahi
      Jo mila h ,usme sabar karo
      Jo nahi mila uske liye sirf Dua karo
      Or khuda ki marzi k mohtaj raho "

ᗡᗡᗡ

" Aaj thak gyi hu ,ruk gyi hu
      Thode waqt baad sambhal jaungi
      Raah-e-ibadat m utha yakeen kayi baar ,
      Toota aitbaar mera
      M phir bhi kayamat m karam azamaungi"

ᗡᗡᗡ

" Khuda bhi muskurata hh
      jab tum uske likhe hue mukaddar se bhi ladte ho
      Or ussi se Fateh ki Dua karte ho
      Or Khuda bhi thak jata h
      Jab tum usse umeed lagana band Kar dete ho
      Or apni shiqast bina lade kabool kar lete ho"

                                        - Sikanda

TWO

FAMILY : MY EXPERIENCE AS AN ADOLESCENT

Fikr karte hain issliye paisa laga rahe hn ya paisa laga rahe hain ... issliye fikr karte hain :: Farq hh

Disclaimer : I don't hate my parents .

Like every other kid ,I also want to see them happy ,want to give them all that they deserve - luxuries ,a big house ,car ,reputation in society and I love them but I don't like them. I don't intend to question their efforts (I am no one to do that) ,I am just producing what I've experienced as a child of this generation... how things went on me .In short ,I hate the way I have been parented.

After spending almost nineteen years of my life with them ,when I crossed that gate to outside world ,I had many painful memories and realizations in my mind ,most of them related to those two years of secondary education - when my anxieties, my fears and my insecurities were active to the most intensity and I ended up as a storeroom of useless thoughts and as a stupid and impractical overthinker .This time ,I think, has and will always have a permanent effect on the way I feel ,the way I see my blood relations and the way I behave I react or behave throughout my age .However mature I grow ,the shades of those days will continue to reflect a rude girl in me and My home now never appears to be what it used to be .

Me and my parents have had differences of opinion since I was twelve or so .I barely agree on their beliefs and vice versa but earlier it was just five or ten minutes that we argued and then be all same .This culture faded away after I entered my eleventh .I distinctly remember being beaten black and blue from my mom whenever I scored less marks or turned ill-mannered sometimes .However ,even then I used to feel resentment but I used to be like- Okkayh!! You are my mom .You can hit me but your slaps should be to make me go right way not using me as a object you using me as a object to vent out all your anger and frustration to satisfy your age ego .I do get physical pain . I am not a wall ,you'll beat me as many sticks as your state of mind demands ,or hit any part of my body - like you can't snatch my hair and pull them with hardness that I fall on floor or you can't put your knee on my neck telling me you have got a right to kill me because I was born from you or you can't twist my elbow and beat me legs ,throw me along my face on wall against any hard surface.

Also, you can't abuse me with all those derogatory words - which I won't even say to my enemies ,those words and your hypothetical statements like :

"Why you were born?"

"My life would be a heaven without you."

"You are just a burden"

"I'd rather be childless than bearing a child like you"

"Girls like you deserve to be raped off ,deserve to be evil eyed"

"Girls like you get sexually exploited by many boys and you'll one day run off with all of them and let me down"

"It is my fault I am paying your school fees ,doing domestic chores ,cooking for you rather what is best is I get your name cut from school ,teach you home - making and marry to a random guy of our caste .This will save both my money and reputation."

This is how I have always been treated by my mom and this kind of thing was not annual or rare like when I had committed some great crime. Infact, I heard all this and have been physically tormented like this whenever I don't agree to her I share my radical ideas (about feminism) or she is bursting out of some issue and my little mistake or voice makes me a criminal and I am automatically a sponge ball!

And after all this she behaves so sweetly like nothing happened not realising will it ever go from my memories. Not only my mother, my father was more cruel .I am one of those unfortunate feminine souls who are not "Papa ki pari" or "Papa ki sherni" rather just "Papa ki zimmedari" - just a responsibility! I don't remember, (not even distinctively) ,when I last played with him ,talked to him forget about hugging or crying in front of him. He is not my hero. I would never like to be like him in my life...never! Though fierce arguments and arguments with him were rare ,but he talked so rashly to me and in anger he has thrown chair on me or dragged me to beat ...his hand was heavy ....he has hit me with his grasp at my head ,in my back and tried to make me things I never wanted to do like complying to his ideas or doing some house chores I hated .Here I would accept that I was lazy kid when it came to domestic work but I am sure this was not the treatment I deserved .He compelled me to be a quiet girl or simply to shut up and bow down to his orthodoxy when I chose to be rebellious and resented .No doubt ,he wished for a son instead of me...especially ME .And he supported my mother and never asked her to change her treatment .I think I'd hurt his male ego.

With many such instances ,I came off as a student of class 11th .Such treatment persisted but now reasons were changed . The cause was not just my ideas but my ideas coming into action .As some teachers of my school began to complain about debates ,arguments and rule breaks who instead of understanding me or discussing with me thought my parents would fix me not knowing it was they who have already broken me . And days passed on with bitter incidences and to that list of statements my mom added some more things like:

"You are characterless."

"You will destroy your life because you didn't opt for science."

"You over react and You are just a dramebaaz ."

"See that guy or that friend of yours who are earning appreciations at such young age and it would be pleasure to be their guardians than yours."

But now I am stronger and mature enough to not expect a fair treatment and kind of emotional support. I will always respect them but also won't ever erase that stuff which broke me into I don't know how many pieces .

As it is said : Family is not everyone's safe place .

Umar k jis padav m itni zindadilli hoti h ki lagta h abhi nahi toh kabhi nahi ,usmein asmaan ki jagah chhat or deewaron m ghutna kya hota h ,ye meri Umar walo se pucho .

I have always hated restrictions like everyone else and I also could see many people of my age getting greater freedom despite belonging to same middle class background. It was just a matter of flexibility or accepting that this age brings excitement, hope, energy, dreams and demands and freedom is (reasonable one) is a requirement of this age .Sometimes ,I don't get this -

Why do parents think restrictions are a teacher of focus ,concentration and stop us from being spoilt ?

Don't we ruin ourselves when loneliness soaks our innocence ,our mental peace and our emotional stability?

How are you protecting us from this cruel world when you can't defend us from YOU ?

How are you ensuring your good bringing up when you are forcing us to be with you and not with healing souls I really want to be with ?t

When will you accept me as an individual and not as your debtor or slave ?

When will change your perception - Giving me space doesn't mean me hiding truths ,letting lies and having relationship and all that ?

When will you accept that having a social life with friends of my choice doesn't mean I will start smoking or drinking or drugs or LOVE ?

When will you see my efforts to become successful and stop seeing other's success - It doesn't motivate me .It kills me .

When will you stop objectifying me, judging me ,finding faults in me ?

When will you stop seeing me through eyes of investment and a forced responsibility?

When will you stop presenting me as a stature of your reputation in society and an answer to 'log kya kahenge' ?

Restrictions aren't cool. They drive us away from ourselves. Its not that we don't care about our careers or that we don't stress ourselves and that we want to destroy our life .But...

How will being happy outside home distract me?

And what is the problem if I spend one or two hours on a ride by my friends or if I go on an yearly trip in a group?

What disaster will it create if I will have a little privacy ? It will just embolden me to take little decisions independently?

And what obsession do you have with - do whatever you want to do after getting successful?

like I won't need your permission if I become successful!

It is now that I need your understanding, your support and you are asking me - Kon kya kahega!!

Why to throw burden of illogical social rules and environment in which you have been brought up ?

The maturity which you had in your forties and fifties ... how do you expect me to have that in my teens ?

Why can't you let me enjoy my age ?

Let me make mistakes ,fall down ,make some wrong choices ... so that I can develop myself in true sense!!

And the way you say - Jab hamari age m aa jaoge tab Pata chalega - like kya pata chalega that having fun in teens is a sin ?

You know ,what we will regret most in our adulthood filled with lots of responsibilities is ki na dhang se jee paye ,na dhang se khush ho paye ,na yaadein ban payi ...

ladte jhagadte waqt beet gaya ,khud k liye kuch na kar paye...

Why can't you let us live these days jo wapas nahi ayenge

Zimmedariyon ka haath thamte thamte pata bhi nahi laga payenge

Chahtein or hasratein m sab kahi kho jayenge ?

You can bind us physically but not our thoughts ,our mind will long for sky and when mental aura is not in line with reality ,it acts like a drug...The more you'll restrict ,the more we will repent our existence and we will develop a haste to maintain a distance from you and you will never be able to measure the miles .We will turn either all silent or all complaining. We lose trust in you. We start doubting your love ,care and concern.

Please stop tying us in iron bails of your fears and overcare about us because darr kisi bhi cheez ka jab tak hi acha rehta h jab tak koi galat kaam karne se roke ,agar rukawat ban raha h toh vo darr nahi veham h.

And we need your care but let us care for ourselves too .Let me spend some time with myself too - learn about me ,accept me with myself and feel Self- love .

The world is poison but stop making me feel homeless who smiles in a house and which is better than poison.

The way you treat, you react ,you force things settle in our heart forever and give us scars -no doctor on this earth can heal ,not GOD even .You make us suffer with trust issues and we are labelled as badtameez ,ghamandi ,laparwah and nalayak because we couldn't live the way you wanted .You could but you didn't let us have our own ways .Maybe, nothing changed for you but my whole belief system about family changed and you didn't even realise .Even after you deny,we will appear happy but what about times jab sirf m thi khud k liye. Only silence knows my screams . You helped me become pale with your complaints ,comparisons and judgements and give me experience of heart breaks from blood relations - you made me realise only three things matter - my marks ,your money and what those people will comment (who don't even matter) over my happiness and over my being okay .

Jo baatien bolke aap soo jate ho ,vo sunke hamein puri raat neend nahi aati .We also get hurt ,feel pain and you justify it all by saying that you care .So ,let generation gap be a gap and not a hollow valley where on my side its all just barren Don't make parenting professional.

DEAR INDIAN PARENTS ,
This is my life too .
You care ,don't control me .

You question ,don't doubt me
You yell ,don't scare me
You opine ,don't judge
You ask ,don't decide
You just say it ,don't tell.
I may be right or wrong
I may rise or fall
I may succeed or fail
I may cry or smile
I may be strong or weak
The world is cruel ,I know
But I'll have to face it on my own
This is what you should know
I don't know everything, I know
But I want to know some things myself
You gave me this life ,I know
But my life has accepted you not me yet
This is what you should know
I will always need you ,I know
But not in front ,at the back
This is what you should know
You have a right in my life ,I know
But I possess my responsibilities on my self too!
This is my life too!

ϷϷϷ

"Main beghar hu kyuki aisi koi jagah hi nahi
Jahan m iss jahan ki zehani thakavat leke jaa saku"

ϷϷϷ

THIS IS HOW GRATEFUL I AM TO MY FAMILY
Your first words were about them
Your first feel was their touch on your soft surface ,that made them overwhelm

Your first music was their prayers praising GOD to send you in their realm

Your first vision was their efforts to make you have a wide smile so that you can be on helm

Your first taste was milk free of toxicity of all pain from which she was not yet over but for you she gave that pain a damn!

It was your birth and their rebirth

They changed everything so that you can be welcomed on this earth

They accepted you as God given grace when you didn't know your worth

They made you an inalienable part of their home and hearth

᭰᭰᭰

"Bahar se jyada samajhdari toh ab Ghar mangne laga hh
Bahar se jyada khof toh mujhe Ghar se aane laga hh
Kam se Kam Bahar meri tanhayi mehfoos toh rehti hh
Ghar pe toh meri rooh mujhse hi Juda rehti hh"

᭰᭰᭰

DEAR DAD ,
    You earned money ,
    While I yearned for company
    You got us accessories ,
    While I also wanted memories
    You were always concerned about fee,
    but I also had to have a family tree
    You are nowhere in my childhood
    and not even now ,isn't it wrong and rude

You are nowhere in my nears and dears
Because you never talked about my fears and tears
You are nowhere in my princess dream,
Because the king always just scream
You helped me in strong built
And you still don't have guilt
I missed imaginary movements I could happily have like a fortunate
Why couldn't you become my mate ?
Your tone and touch is hard ,harder than you work ,so hard to hurt my heavy heart
But now it's all a past part!!
"Rishton ko khush karne k liye kamate ho
Par tumhari kamayi k baad bhi koi kami Hai
Itna waqt nahi nikal pate ho?
Dil ka haal sudhar nahi jata mehaz
Jeb m pade sikkon k shor se
Par tumhari ek Awaaz... sabak ki or ehsaas ki
Azaad kar deti hh ek unchahe bojh"

- Sikanda

THREE

ANGER AND SELF RESPECT

Anger ,I think is the most pure and also one of the most violent emotions of human existence. The most expressive one .Anger is sometimes like fire in a volcano which burns everything - relations ,memories and respect. Other times ,it is like evaporation of frustration and the rain washes off all misunderstandings ,complaints and confusions .

Controlling your anger is the greatest self control one can possess .The basic reason of anger is - things around you not accordingly to you .It is manifested in many ways - abusing the other person ,breaking objects into pieces ,destroying the environment or hurting yourself .

I think this is just a way of escaping tears for some people who can't let weakness out of their eyes and thus they choose to release it all through tongue and toxicity rather eyes .

Earlier ,it was said that those who can't act strong ,cry! but now those who can't handle pain instead of forgetting and leaving it for loneliness ,frustrate themselves.

Best part about anger is it can't persist for too long and is a characteristic of moody people .The speed it picks up to reach it's peak ,same is for the voice and hike of emotions to come to normality .And it is one of those conditions - when the person is true ,real himself - all masks removed - whatever he says is honest because the mind to modify or manipulate the words doesn't work and the person is in all grasp of heart.

But remember ,anger is just a reaction to disliked surroundings and actions of people around ,it can still be kept in check .Your anger switches off chill mode and triggers serious mode and your expectation of others being serious about the same thing results in your inability to figure out the situation with calmness and simple conversations. Well ,I do agree sometimes it's inevitable and there are some genuine issues you just break out on the other person because you are too hurt to leave it for later .

Anyways ,anger helps you classify people -

Jo chahe kitne hi gusse m ho , (not necessarilynbecause of you) , they just say - abhi dimak

bohot kharab h terse baad m baat karta hu - who don't want to spoil your mood and

Jo tum chahe kitne hi gusse m ho ,tumhari sunte hn no matter tum kitna unreasonable sound kar rhe ho yaa kitna hi over reacting appear ho rhe ho , jo tumhe samajhte hn or tum (unwillingly) kitna hi bura behave kar rhe ho,they'll be with you ,take you to some other place just to stop you being a drama in front of everyone .

You realise this classification after the matter is over and you sit silently to analyse what scene you had created when you were high with emotions ,

Don't only find and preserve these two types of people but be one of those people for someone you truly have got to be with .Those who handle themselves to not be a burden on you and those who handle you when you are burden on them- their presence determine how lucky you are .

Anger is not always healthy. I believe anger is of two types- positive anger and negative one.

Positive Anger is kind of emotional resentment .It arises when you have been swallowing up so many things inside you, since long ,disturbing your mind again and again and you are trying hard to get normal or that it doesn't come up. But then a sudden incident opens up the vent and long molten memories piss you off to utter out the facts that have been hurting and you told no one just not to spoil it for everyone else .You lose control of your mind and tongue. Only your heart is speaking that was saved for silent battles .Your manners ,etiquettes burn somewhere in that air and later you regret with your weight off heart. But this was all natural.

Negative anger is kind of egoistic, cleverly mined scene .It doesn't arise ,it is made to occur as a revenge because not your heart but your ego is hurt. You are not driven by emotions but your expectations that others do need to do as you say just because you are at a particular position or exercise authority. You don't care about reasonability or relevance ,just because YOU BELIEVE IT ,EVERYONE SHOULD . You intend to force things and thus willingly, you say those things to other person ,which will definitely hurt him. You blame him for your faults. Only your mind works because you believe the other person will listen to your shit as he so called...respects you . This ego can be on the virtue of age,money or reputation.

This only satisfied your ego ,you created a scene ,defamed someone ,played with your rules and left the ground. You don't realise the other person (though materially not as equivalent to you) still possess self respect as you do.

So ,don't let your ego consume you Everyone has got some achievements and everyone deserves to be respected simply by virtue of being a human being .

If I personalize a little bit from my experiences - I believe that there is a line which no one ,absolutely NO ONE ,can cross neither for joke nor in anger .I am not short tempered but I get irritated easily with things I can't compromise on for sure and when ,I get like seriously angry, I dissappear from ears of people and open up to walls of a closed room .I may behave bitter and tend to break anything I see and come out normal after I open the door.

When I am angry ,I say facts ,I realise fakeness and I also remind myself of the frequency in which I've been hurt because of the same issue and question- Will things ever change?

How long will I have to hear all this and feel that uncontrolled fire ?And when I am done with doubts and I close the matter in silence with a little statement- Why do I get affected from from somethings and to the same intensity everytime ?But I don't feel sorry or regret for all my reactions but just a little thought ki cheezen alag ho sakti thi but the entire thing was not at all my fault. Others pointed me pins of words that dropped directly into my heart and then my later behavior was just a con commitent and spontaneous .Unless my heart pricks, I won't argue I was right .

Because in India ,koi nahi dekhta apko kaise treat Kiya gaya ,aap hurt hue ,apke character pe question Kiya gaya ,apki integrity ko kuchla gaya ,apki self respect ko Ronda gaya for a very silly reason ki aap umar m ya rishte m chhote ho ,lekin apne kaise react kiya vo ultimately buri parvarish or badtameezi ho jati h .

Trust me when I say this - it is very easy to say - vo toh Hai hi muphat ,vo toh Hai hi besharam ,iske liye toh kisi ko kuch karna hi nahi chahiye but you don't know how much courage it takes to be the only one to understand yourself ,to respect yourself, to accept your faults and loopholes ,to justify yourself and to take a stand for yourself. So ,if someone can't get you and is meant to just judge You without knowing the whole thing or isn't curious about your damn personal life ,they deserve to be answered back.

Self respect is pillar of dignified existence ,a backbone pf behaviour- sensitive but strong one and if someone recognise and respect you , you need not consider age or relation. (I don't honestly !) . I can't tolerate disrespect from anyone .The respect which I've built myself, a strength I gained when I was alone doesn't depend on anyone validating it on the grounds of whether I earn or don't earn but I derive it for myself on the basis of my Individuality and as member of Mighty Human Kingdom everyone is equally part of.So, anger is not evil - sometimes it is requirement of situation.

Anger isolates you but makes it clear too who comes to break that isolation ,who knows you are not wrong you are hurt and thus makes you feel confident .Anger involves many people and you later find role of your people.And I must say there must be a limit to

your tongue as well ,your words may not be perfect but careful ...
it shouldn't appear like you have got a license just because you are
hurt ,you will hurt everyone else immeasurably .

Now coming to the last facet of anger that is staying calm .Must
be sounding funny but nothing and no words can match the power
of peaceful silence - when you just don't care who says what or
thinks what... You are into yourself .

If you can stay calm when you can say a lot as you felt a lot ,then
you have won over heart ,you have learnt to tame your mind and
control factors in your environment. In short ,you have won a major
battle of your life and earned tolerance and acceptance and come to
terms with " Not everyone can get you " .You don't like attention and
let the people or situations be the way they are meant to be.

This staying calm has always been linked with MATURITY - a
trait of the understanding, a characteristic of the cool and involves
many undermined struggles ,compromises and sacrifices . Maturity
hits you when you think ...Har baar confront karna zaroori nahi
hota ,jisse samajhna hota h vo samajh jata h .You start having
essence of silence .You develop walls around you and no instigation
can make you break that ,no provocation can make you jump over
the height you have set for yourself .It requires lots of patience
to exercise that kind of self control .And no doubt ,such maturity
comes with age ,gradually, you know ,when you have had enough
fights, arguments and disagreements ,clashes and conflicts and you
realise you derive nothing out of violent encounters except mental
imbalance and emotional disturbance .This realisation marks your
road to silence .Maturity needs efforts ,you put yourself in a
different aura .

Conclusively ,It would be wrong to clearly determine what is
right- reacting the way your heart says or the way your experiences
tell .You are not wrong both ways .For me, there are some things
I fight about and no settling down can reverse - the issue is not
whether the comment or judgement given by person opposite to me
is right or wrong but why was that statement even said !!

While with my age ,I am also learning- itni badi baat bhi nahi hh .Stuck between both these...my heart ,my body ,my mind ,my actions and reactions are directed always to find What is the most practical and desirable way I can go and many search is on.I think you need to be different as the difference of situation demands .No theory is entirely perfect or always right.

When I am angry ...
    When dark ,happy pictures are burning inside
    I tend to ignite everything outside

A sudden release of energy like a high tide
Through the hot ambiance into my limbs from each side
I just vomit loudly all what uselessly I had sorted and behave wild
I may be killing something but it's high time I didn't
My silence turns into violence but I am a victim ,whose pains are you think ,too mild
Look into my eyes then ,you'll know , they have got dried
My heart has absorbed all moisture but sometimes even emotions have to abide
When this loo comes in contact with a cool breeze ,everything melts and on the bed of smoothness ...It just get slide

ϷϷϷ

" Mere lehje se taleem -e- tameez ki mehak sirf
Kisi guroor m gumshuda se takra jaane k pehle tak aati hh
Uske baad taluq or tarbiyat dono mere raste se hatt jaati hh
Berukhi or Badtameezi ki bardasht nahi bakshi Khuda ne
ana m phirne walo ki hadd or aukat dono yaad Dilani aati hh
Apni shan ka elan tum khud se muntasir mehfil m karna
Apne dil ki janasheen toh m hu
Mujhe har suluk ki aziyat lautani aati hh"

ϷϷϷ

"Kisi ki Ana se jab takrao toh usse uski hadd dilani zaroori hh
Par baat jab kisi ki ghairat pe aaye ,toh mazak ho ya gussa
Maafi maang lo Yahin tumhari tarbiyat puri hh"
Pov : when you are asked to compromise on your principles
"Aaj usulon ko chhod k kuch chunna hh
Akhir pure mustaqbil ka sawal
Par haalat-e-dil kehta h ..
kamyabi ki chah h mujhe
Par meri ibadat har chahat-e-zindagi se badi hh"

ϷϷϷ

" Jyada mushkil nahi hh
Kisiki galtiya chantna
Kisiki kamiya pesh karna
Kisike daur-e-aziyat m saza sunake ek taraf ho jana
Par asaan nahi hh
Kisike zehan-e-zakham pe ek khamosh aitbar karna
Na puche hue sawalon ka sabr se intezar karna"

- Sikanda

FOUR
TRUST AND EXPECTATIONS

When anger is all about expression ,trust is about kind of unsaid ,delicate string of bond which gets strengthened over time. Trust is the basis of all bonds we get or make in life ;without this ,no blood relation ,no Friendship ,no love can survive .Without trust ,the relation is just a hollow pipe connecting two people .Trust acts like oxygen to otherwise meaningless ,show off formalities one is bound to perform living in society i.e. just as lifeless burden .Having trusted people around and people who trust you adds colour to life of responsibilities.

My experience in life tell me about two types of trust ... like two ways you trust ... on the basis of basis of depth and intensity-

One is you diverge a secret to someone you feel close to and expect that the secret won't turn into a gossip to the third person and you don't tell that thing to share some information but the weight was too heavy that you decided to share that weight .When your this action doesn't come come out as a mistake ,it is a testimony you trusted the right one .And you may have few people in your life of such sort . But I think this is just a ground for deeper type of trust which is not limited upto secrets or some difficult moments or just expectation. This trust is bolder and realised after years of being together ,after facing many problems together and after being a witness to circumstances with each - other.

And in my words I define it : "Chahe duniya idhar se udhar ho jaye ;

Saare log, saare rishte khilaf ho jaye ;

Kitna hi bada toofan zindagi m aa jaye ;

Zindagi puri tehas nehas ho jaye ;

Vo ek insaan jo apka saath kabhi nahi chhodega

Hamesha apko andhere m bhi Chirag dikhayega

Apko mazboot or khush rakhega

Or jab Zamane se tumhara amna samna hoga

Vo ek insaan tumhare saath khada rahega

Tumhe darne nahi dega

Tumhe akela padne nahi dega "

"Aisa nahi h ki aise log zindagi m Kam hote hn

balki bohot Kam logon ki zindagi mein aise log hote hn"

It is very difficult to discover diamond in sand !

If you have ,even one such soul or if you have the courage to be one for your someone ; label yourself as one of the luckiest beings .

The nuclie of this trust is who trusts you and not whom you trust like the former.

Developing such trust ,such comfort level is gradual and comes up only when such situation arises .

This person may not have the solution to your problems but his very existence in life in that way would compel you to find medicine ,to embolden and have belief in yourself .Such person is a blessing for you who understands your silence ,your circumstances and your anger. Not everyone has got a good luck to possess a soul through which ,may be , GOD send you lots of love ,care and support .So ,hold their hands tightly if you have one.

When we are into trust ,another term clicks - BLIND TRUST - means putting a blockade to your senses and even your common sense and solely believing the other person which is highly unreasonable and mature .Blind trust is like being drunk - You don't have a logic or you don't find a reason to just agree to what the other person says or does and you justify it in the name of FRIENDSHIP

OR LOVE . Such trust is best ,I have seen ,meant for some selfish agenda either on your part or on the other side and is meant to be broken once the purpose is met. Don't trust anyone more than yourself ...it can prove to be self destructive.

When someone trusts you ,it doesn't mean he will always say 'You are right!' When you are right ,he will take your side but when you are wrong he'll fight against you for you and with you .He'll argue, he'll anyhow prove in what way your wrongness is identified (though not in front of any third person) .When you are right ,he will stand behind you to not let you fall down and let you charge on your own battles ,but when you are wrong ,he will be the first one to help you mend your ways .Whose righteousness and wrongness doesn't depend on what people will say ? Or what image will it cast but only on what is desirable ? Or his entire focus be on your happiness .

When someone trusts you he will never hurt your self respect but attack your ego again and again unless that shatters down; he won't appreciate if you do something so called cool but will give you rude reality checks until you realise it .

When someone trusts you ,he will reach your comfortable mental and emotional level and sincerely tell you -" I am not against you ,I am against what may destroy you within you and I am always there to look at your actions objectively look at your actions .I am not a judge so please don't justify as a lawyer .And I will always trust you ... since I have known you to a greater depth .And I know you can never hurt someone intentionally but at some places ,you emerge wrong " and he proves his words alongwith different dark and light days of life .

One more dimension that needs to be highlighted is don't let your trust be faked off by hypocrisy .Like my parents say they trust me but they also keep a check on my phone, also restrict me from being with my friends and tell me ki maine abhi duniya dekhi nahi hh and under this title they take all my decisions on my behalf .

They say they trust me but when it comes to support me in front of this world ,forget about supporting ,they blame me believing those relatives or neighbors and outsiders .

They say they trust me but don't let me go alone or with friends they have lesser known .

They also say I should trust them and then if I tell them some unpleasant happening in my friendship or relationship life ,they dismiss it as an emotional hoax and start judging me,finding faults in me ,blaming me for being happy and then to focus only on my career .I don't know what is all this called - a family with widened generation gap or so .

If they trust me ,they should only trust me about me and my matters ,they should listen to my life through my words too.

If they trust me ,they should open the ceiling of my house so that I can create my home in sky ,let me set my own limits and dive into an air of little chillness mixed with career seriousness.

If they trust me,they should let me be on my own and let me develop some self trust.

If they trust me ,they shouldn't overfear and overthink that I'll be easily driven to smoke ,to drink or drive or engage in a relationship; they should believe that I can refuse too , I am not a socially stupid soul ,that even I have career priorities.

Its not about their right on me ,it's about my space in my life .By not trusting me ,they just make me down my self worth .

If they trust me ,I shouldn't be telling lies ,hiding truths and tears ,faking smile over thousands of problems because I didn't get space in house so I made a vacuum in my heart and such family experiences have made me dig deep holes and burry those expectations from a happy family life .

A form of trust is also SILENT TRUST means when your life and heart is experiencing a total hustle and bustle and everyone is just bothering and you are turning into a confused corner , there is someone who definitely trusts you and try to not question you and even if they do ask ,it is when they don't find another way to help you after they have silently waited for you to open up to them ,who actually says - tu itna galat nahi ho sakti! kuch toh baat h! Silent trust is a really mature and understanding feeling you can experience in your bad time by virtue of that silent truster .

If after all these generalizations, what it reflects when I say 'my trust' ,it'd be a bit particularised .MY TRUST has to be like a transparent window glass - strong and clear .If someone tells me all his secrets ,his feelings, his instabilities ,anger issues and about incidences which shaped him the way he is without any patches of hidden things (if you trust me completely) ,without any fear of being judged and if this trust remains untouched from any third party (I hate intervention of third things) ,then I'll say I trust someone.

It takes me,may be months to trust someone even for little things (I don't have levels of trust - no translucency- either opaque or transparent) but when I do ,you'll see a different version of me - my craziness ,stupidities and child like things, my pains I have hidden for so long ,my strengths and weaknesses and even if some problem arises ,I'll make efforts because it was my decision to trust you but even if once I see a little scratch on that glass ,I'll break the entire glass into pieces myself .My kind of trust is hard to understand and it may appear impractical but I can't let down my standards about trust.

How it feels when you are betrayed?

This is one of the most painful reality shocks in the life .Fault appears not on their part ,but YOU .You blame yourself for your innocence and niaveness to see through people's plan .You are broken. You lose the courage to even trust yourself again .You are afraid of this world now .The pieces, you will find hard to pick up ,will seem to laugh at you and you don't know how to behave or react or think or feel. Each piece will give you permanent lessons to not believe in any promises .Your thoughts will leave you ,your mind will curse your heart and your soul mutes itself. You begin doubting not only your decision making but also those days when you were happy .You complain to GOD and pray to not grant you wishes once you had asked .You start looking your other trustworthy people unclearly. You ask everyone to leave from your life and most deep spike is one which was used for attack by people naturally meant to be trusted like family or blood relations because there is no one to handle if someone your own breaks you ,no one can heal you then.

Trust is password of heart and your entire existence can be hacked eternally if went in wrong hands!!

The most evident and bottom step of trust is EXPECTATIONS. To simply say ,expectations are your hope in darkest times that things will get better with time ,it is leaving the matter on other side ,when you think you have done enough. It is putting some responsibility of you on the other person or on the situation to be in your favour.

As it is trending on social media - Don't expect anything from anyone!! I believe this is not possible. Yes! expectations expose you to get more hurt but if these expectations are fulfilled ,you become the happiest .Expectations are not negative but they are natural .

How can you not expect them two steps for you when you have walked miles for them?

How can you not expect them to not make you smile and brighten your days when you have spent nights crying for them?

How can you not expect them to justify you in front of some unknown when you took their stand in front of your closed ones ?

How can you not expect them to live some moments with you when you left your life for them?

Not expecting is cool but not pragmatic. And please determine the difference between expectations and demands .Demands are selfish while expectations just hope of them recognising your efforts , wanting them to realise your worth and to realise what you deserve on their part and wishing that they make some gestures for you .Expectations arise from your desire of your efforts being reciprocated .Reciprocation ensures a flow of give and take and keeps one from reaching to one - sidedness realisation in conclusion .Though not fifty - fifty but eighty - twenty is a necessity .

So ,don't put expectations in some dark space and also don't force these expectations. Don't let your beautiful expectations be a burden on someone. If they are not interested in Increasing any involvement, all changing upto some angles .

Don't go farther and you start declining your active energies in that direction .

Not expecting doesn't give you peace ,it just helps you put curtain on colours of life and light as you are afraid of view not being as beautiful as you.

I do agree after a certain age ,you will lose interest in yourself making efforts but teens or twenties is not that age.

Trust and Expectations are a double sided coin and it depends on fate and many other apparent factors ,so its hard to determine if you'll get the favourable side. And do not stop trusting because you got hurt once .

Sometimes ,giving second chances isn't getting hurt more severely rather helping yourself heal from previous pain.

EXPECTATIONS

You find yourself under mountain of doubts
You can't see what this riddle in mind is all about
Millions of questions attacking the mind ruthlessly in loud
You become quiet and try to find some safe and sorted cloud
You approach a more aged one to nicely negotiate
But he presents a new unpleasant picture of you and you don't retaliate
This same stays and repeats...these exertions don't allow you to elevate

You hold your hand and see where your life is heading obviously not towards goal its something immediate

You change the wind ,your boat gets separated from others ,now you have some comfort

You don't have any barriers to your dream you are free of all dirt

No one to assign you a new star of responsibility or to demand a sacrifice only to make you hurt

No one to judge You if you fail to fill the full of their expectations from you but do stay alert

As no one on whom you can throw stones of your thoughts ,learn to lift the loss or profit of loneliness and wear your own shirt

ᐳᐳᐳ

"Yakeen vo ki khula asmaan bhi tumhare liye khol den

Or phir bhi na tumhare kho Jane ka or na tumhare vapas na aane ka khof ho

Na tumhare or toofano k takra jaane pe tumhari shiqast ka shaqq ho

Log kahenge ye gair zimmedari h

Par nahin ! Ye galat baaton ki nafarmai or kisi ki udaan ki zimmedari h"

ᐳᐳᐳ

"Sabooton ka baad toh gair bhi maan jate hn

Apne toh vo hote hn jo Bina tumhare kuch kahe tumhari khamoshi pe jaan dete hn"

ᐳᐳᐳ

" Jhooth ka hi sahi par ye parda jaane kitno ka yakeen kayam rakhe hua h

Lekin parde ki bhi ek umar hh akhir isse bhi toh insaano ne wajood diya hua h

Aine k upar bicha ye parda ,jis din hatega dono taraf tukde hi tukde honge

Emaan , umeed or haqeeqat sab dubi hui rooh se chilla rahe honge "

ÞÞÞ

"Sabke apne fayde hain par rooh k uss par kon dekh paya hh
Tameez ,lehja or khayal ek shaqsiyat hn...ab nazar -e- fareb inhe bhi dhak deti hh
Iss daur-e-andhere mein kaha kisiko haqeeqat pasand hh
Kisne aaj tak mukhote pehchanne k baad kuch acha paya hh"

ÞÞÞ

" Meri hifazat Karni h toh asmaan ko buri nazron se azaad karao
Par meri udaan pe pabandiya mat lagao
Kyuki kaid mein m beshaq khatron se bahar hu
Par dil mehfooz nahi h
Inn fikr ki bediyo ko Zara hatao"

- Sikanda

FIVE

HAPPINESS AND SELF -LOVE

Why do we need trusted people around ?Isn't it obvious...so that they can make us happy after discovering sadness ?Happiness is a success no one acknowledges ,a staircase to life in true sense no one cares to climb and a strength e eryone needs but no one marks it important. Happiness is a failure of your fate and victory of GOD. It is when you don't bother yourself for things you don't want to think ,when you don't push yourself for what is against your heart and mind and when you pull positivities .

Happiness isn't a mood for some moments or a stage of life ,it is a nature and parcel of existence. It isn't when you not apparently crying or shouting or it isn't when you are just neutral or normal...rather it is when you can transit yourself from this world to the world you have created within yourself and create a kind of permanent passage of only your thoughts.

To think , it is just smiles and laughter or any of your wish being fulfilled but to feel, it's an entirely different vision you see your life with and it isn't getting careless or so...its just caring in a different way .Happiness is when your heart agrees to your mind and both develop a bond, a simple one to assist you .Happiness is hope that lets you smile in darkness because you are certain of light ,is faith that everything must be going fair and you are just unaware of some factors in fairness and is a higher level of increasing your standards rather than expectations ,it is discovering easiness of life in some way.

But Khushi jitni zaroori hh utni hi mushkil bhi .Its hard to be happy and maintain this happiness throughout. Happiness has got to be with you like a handle of heart and you being the driver not the problems or situations - Don't let it fade away like you don't throw your favourite flower plant after the spring is gone. In fact ,what you do is you may change its position or now you may need to water it more frequently because you know it will blossom beautifully some day ,you know seasons are meant to change but not your choices which you regard favourite .And whatever season it is , it will continue to decorate a corner of your house and to brighten your days .

Don't let happiness be like wind ,make it air .Winds are meant to come, stay and go but air is meant to persist in all landscapes, reliefs and soils equally.

Make happiness as intrinsic part of your life as a night....in days ,it may be sunny or rainy or cloudy but nights are always cooler ,same throughout no matter how the day was and let your hope be the moon. Sunlight is dependant on weather while moonlight is independent...so make it happy dark .No doubt ,moon has phases but all nights are so common and such commonality is difficult in days .And this feeling , these efforts need to be preserved .

So, protect your flower ,your air and your nights from your moods and stages and let these fill the vacuum that got created inside you .Dig them into deep holes of walls in pain but just dig ,don't bury. Don't you think it is a necessity to not compromise on yourself when it comes to YOU deep down?

You need not win this world to attain that nature of happiness ,only little things and your attitude towards them can turn things for you . Chhoti chhoti khushiyan jaise koi chhota bacha khelte hue dikh jana ,jo alarm set Kiya thha uss par bina kisi shikanj k uth pana ,pasand ka khana mil jana ,jisse bohot time se baat nahi hui h uska unexpectedly call aa jana ,kahi bahar ho toh kudrat ka koi khubsurat nazara dekh pana ,jiss baat par roz daant padti thhi ,aaj uss galti k liye chhod diya jaana, achanak se zindagi m kuch haasil karne ka khayal aa jana ,ek sundar sa knwab neend m aana ,kisi apne se jhagde k baad tumhe manane k liye uska koshish karna ya tum koshish karo or uska maan jana ,jo hamesha tumhe sunta rehta h uski ek hansi dekh lena ,tumhare kiye hue mazak par sabka dil kholke hasna ,kisi ki madad kar pana ,kisi ki duaon m shamil hona ,waqt se pehle koi kaam khatam kar lena ,kisi se halki si tumhari tareef sun lena, dost ki kisi harkat mein uski dosti ka saboot mil jana ,kisi fikr se fariq ho jana or aise hazaron lamhe jo pura dil or din khush kar dete hain.

Khushi vo nahin h jab sab kuch tumhare hisab se chal raha h balki tab h jab jo tumhe socha Tha haalat usse alag bhi hon or behtar bhi ,jab ek jhatke mein tum apni takleefen bhul jaate ho or sab kuch thik lagne lagta h . Shayad kuch hi lamho ka vo manzar hota h par pura din bana deta h .Or khushi zehan mein honi chahiye varna tum kuch bhi haasil kar lena- chahe ye puri duniya tumhari sharton pe chalne lag Jaye, tumhe faraq nahi padega .Jab tak tumhare dil mein khush hone ki ;Khushi dhundhne ki chahat nahi hogi , tumhare liye hasna bhi mushkil ho jayega.

Jab tak asmaan nahi dekhna chahoge ,zameen se Bahar kaise aaoge ? Baat mijaz ki nahi h just that aap apna pichla mood bhul jate ho or lamho ki hawaon k saath chal dete ho .

Then nowadays ,there is a thing that maturity means not getting happy anymore ,not letting little things affect your seriousness .I find this sentence itself immature .

Haa...jab baarish mcin bhigte ho ,baag se koi sundar phool tod late ho ,apne dil ki koi baat muhphat ban k bol dete ho ,jo tumhe apna lagta h uske liye bhid jate ho ya apni hi koi buri aadat bss yuhi bayan kar dete ho yaa jo cheez logo ko pasand na ho or tum ussi cheez pe itrate ho toh log tumhe 'pagal 'kehte hn.

This generation has developed a contradiction between Happiness and maturity but my stand is jyada samajhdar hona bhi koi samajhdari ki baat nahi . So, don't loose your childhood still existing inside you to become an adult or a cool Adolescent. Agar logon ki Khushi k liye tum apni khushiyon ki khudkushi karoge toh ye bevakoofi hogi or logo ko nahi apne aap ko or Khuda ko khush karne ki socho .Kyuki log toh kabhi khush nahi honge or kya iss chakkar m tum khud ko bhi na khush rakhoge .Asli samajhdari duniya ko nazarandaz karne mein hh. Agar logon ki jyada sunoge toh khud ki kabhi nahi sun paoge .Toh khush hona zaroori hh dil vo haryali honi chahiye ...'ek perfect person' k tag m fit hona itna bhi zaroori nahi hh .

Or hasne mein or khush hone mein kya farq h ye samjhna jyada mushkil nahi hh

Sheeshe mein or naqab mein kya farq h ye Janna koi bada masla nahi hh .

Remember , it's not everyone's cup of tea to be literally happy .And you know? Why we don't want to be happy sometimes? The reason is we are scared of its temporariness .Hum log zindagi bhar permanence k peeche bhagte rehte hn. We are scared that after a few moments ,it will go... so let it go .But jab tak uss moment ka affect tumhare upar hh tab tak toh rehne do . Don't get scared to get SAD .

Kya 'marna h' ye soch k hum jeena chhod dete hain ?

Ya phir 'raat ho jayegi',ye soch k din m dukhi ho jate hain?

Ya phir saare paise ek din khatam ho jayenge ,ye soch k paise kamana or Kharch karna band Kar dete hain?

Nahin na! Kyuki hamen pata h ki maut badli nahi jaa sakti par zindagi ka tareeka badla jaa sakta hh .Har subah ki raat hoti h par raat bhi subah se Juda nahi h ...isse kudarat ka Karishma kaha jaa sakta hh. Paise ki fitrat hh aate jate rehna or ye kabiliyat k dam par phir se kamaya jaa sakta hh .Toh gam phir aayega ...ye khushi har pal ki haqeeqat nahi hogi ..toh ye sab soch kar zehan phika kyu karna ,khushiyon ko khud se door kyu rakhna ?

Or agar khushiyan hamesha k liye nahi h toh gam or dard bhi toh qayamat tak m liye nahi h n!

And one more thing I have to highlight is ...some people say..."I used to be happy!"

Matlab ek waqt Tha jab tum sab kuch Sambhal lete thhe yaa jab kuch sambhalne ki zaroorat nahi hoti thhi .Jab tumhare upar bojh nahi tha issliye tum khud ka dhyan rakh lete the .

Ab mushkil lagta hh . Ab khud ko tum kahi piche chhod aaye ho or jism lekar zimmedariyon k neeche bhage jaa rhe ho. Par kya tum apne saath insaaf kar rahe ho ?

Why don't you drag it from your past ?

Why don't you let those days and their essence still last ?

Why don't you make your same mind and heart as you had and in you now life, make a happy blast?

I know it's easier said rather done .Easy to remind ourselves of past ,but difficult to forget present. But let me tell you..you can still be happy ! You can still have that glow in your smile. What all you need is forget the distance of past from present and connect them while making them respect each other and making a beautiful combo and then happily running after future .There is a difference between being careless and being carefree. The former is irresponsibility and the latter is not letting responsibilities kill you .

Isn't it lovely of you going to chase your dreams not forcefully but freely?

Isn't it lovely of you taking care of your little needs and smiles and other people reciprocating?

Isn't it lovely you making your today a happy yesterday for the coming tomorrow ?

I find two levels of happiness existing ...on the basis of its origin ,effects and permanence. One is which treats your heart like a public place like coming and going as per changing circumstances. It distracts your mind of current mental or emotional situation. It is a medicine which is there or not doesn't make a difference. It'll just cause a little tide and then you'll come back to normality and realise reality .It is just a smell which may have a little longer impact if you want to retain it but it will vanish in air after some time .The source of this happiness can be friends or family or a trip or something you were waiting for and expecting to last for some time.

The other is which treats your heart like a security zone area ,carefully monitored .This stays in your heart forever as a protector and rescues you when things are not happening. It doesn't change and is permanent . It always keeps a check and remove all the unwanted stress and to some extent ...saves you from anxiety and overthinking too. This happiness lasts to motivate and provide a relief .Whatever problem you are going through, as you will enter this arena of your heart...there will be peace and positivity .It is the reason of you keep heading forward in hope when this happiness acts as torch .It doesn't vanish in air ,it amasses all fresh air into your heart windows .It isn't smell ,it is an aura in itself .This happiness is intensified with time and experience. It doesn't let you lose you .

This happiness teaches you something- Don't make your smile sensitive ,but make its existence real and hard .If little things can make you laugh some other unexpected seconds can also make you ruin everything. Don't make it a mistake to be happy. Don't let it be easily driven away or dissappear from your face ,but store it .Make your smile of a fatter skin , make it fight for itself and don't let your smile easily give up. Happiness is no less than success in life game .You lose, you learn, you let yourself live and the script of life heads on .

Make happiness an applied practical philosophy not theory at functions or festivities.

SO , LETS MAKE HAPPINESS A CULTURE ,SMILE A SPIRIT AND THIS LIFE A HAPPY PLACE .

This generation has made happiness just a time waste not realising real time waste is when they are faking smile and making a joke of this life .

Last dimension and most important element of happiness is SELF LOVE - a popular term with incomplete understanding and an unpopular reality .Self love doesn't shape your attitude ,it marks your personality .Self love is prioritizing your own priorities over anyone else's, is not considering everyone worthy of explanations and justifications ,is realising self- worth ,is creating a space around you where you wander all around ,is searching for real happiness ,is focusing on your real mental health ,is trusting people very carefully, is possessing the ability to understand yourself when no one does ,is mastering the art of balancing between YOU ;career and family , is trying to shake hands with past peacefully ,is giving time to yourself so that your wounds heal and taking up yourself .And this all is not a left hand thing. It may appear easy but hard to stop yourself from being too kind or available, to instruct yourself at making different layers of trust and treating people accordingly and to create boundaries.

Self love is your own thing ..so, OWN it! Self love is also about feeling proud of the way you are carrying your mistakes ,loop holes ,not so good habits and counting on small daily achievements and appreciating it and still striving to be more co- operative and accountable to your goals rather than society . Self love is putting a mirror and it is better than seeing yourself through other's lens .It is a different plane than self obsession which can be defined as ignoring your faults and instead of correcting them, justifying them to be cool and inviting attention and looking at yourself as someone from different class than people around you.

A misconception about self love is that it is hyper independence and that you don't need anyone else .Self Love is fulfilling own needs and being as less dependable for your moods ,care and stability as you can do it on your own and not looking anyone else's role in life or denying their rights in your life .You will always need other people ,you can't isolate but that need must not make you stand at their door .When something triggers you or troubles you ,you may right a diary and then spill out to someone you are closest to you in family or in friends group and like crying alone and sharing the story later is self love but over - confidence about suffering alone and faking your behaviour and not letting anyone is self obsession (your image as a strong ,mature person may get ruined).

So,self love is maturity and I must say ,is not natural rather there are some incidences after which you learn to love yourself too - after you get betrayed or get mistreated or you feel suffocated in forced unhappy social life or you develop self respect - then you learn a lot about yourself.

Happiness and Self love make you achieve life ,so achieve it before you achieve your dream.

YOU ,YOURSELF
    Don't hate , love yourself
    Don't let blame , advocate yourself
    Don't hurt , heal yourself
    Don't question, answer yourself
    Don't doubt ,trust yourself
    Hate your haters ,live for love
    Blame their judgements, advocate your opinions
    Hurt your pains, heal your soul
    Question your complaints, answer back your hope

Doubt your fate ,trust your actions and intentions!!

ᐅᐅᐅ

"Gair zaroori maslon par gor farmana
Be matlab zehan ko khayalon se azmana
Phir paglon si harkaton k baad khud ko aaina dikhana
Bss kabhi kabhi khud ko aaj se kho dena"

ᐅᐅᐅ

"Kitni galtiyan ki ,kitna kuch galat hua
Kitni saari khushiyan mili ek hansta khelta jhomta dil hasil hua
Kabhi fiza si khubsurati dekhi toh kabhi saza sa waqt paya
Zindagi ka harr marahil dekh paya
Itni si zindagi m itna hi paya"

ᐅᐅᐅ

"Zindagi chhoti nahi hh
Har pal guzarta yuhi nahi hh
Ek ek pal k kayi tukde hn
Kisi m sukoon or sirat toh
Kisi m sawal, sitam or samjhauta bhi kahi hh
Upar wala umar m ye din nahi
Inn tukdon m jiye ehsaas ginta hh
Anjaam m na mauka milta h na mohlat
Sirf lagta h mukaddar sahi h "

ᐅᐅᐅ

"Ghanto tak tarazoo m tola har pal ko hamne
Na jaane kitne lamhe nakamyabi se
Khuda ka kaam karte karte yuhi barbad kar diye hamne"

ᐅᐅᐅ

"Ek pal aaya or meri saari shikayaten le gaya
Dil maano azaad ho gaya
Mere liye hawa ki uss bahar se

chhin k saari muskurahat mujhe de gaya"

"Kadar karo apne har andaaz ki
Sivaay uske jo sache dil ko dard de
Tumhare khayal or sawaal alag hi sahi
Par bemissal hain
Aqidat rakho apni paak rooh pe
Bss Dua karo ye zamana tumhe aise hi rehne de
Tum Khuda ko aise hi ache lagte ho "

"Tumhe tumse jyada or koi nahi janta
Tumhare andar ka vo shaqs koi aaina nahi pehchanta
Apne aap se Zara guftagu kiya karo
Apna ehtiram kiya karo
Apne aap ko mazbooti se pesh kiya karo
Karte honge log fikr tumhari
Par khud se jyada unpe aitbar mat Kiya karo"
"Khud ko khud k saath rakho
Kisi ladne wale se toh beshaq jeet jaoge
Par agar jism k andar Jung shuru ho gyi
Ek ek pal ki muskurahat ka intezaar
tum sadiyo tak karne m majboor ho jaoge"

- Sikanda

SIX
FRIENDSHIP AND SOCIAL LIFE

Just as family stands between you and society, Friendship holds your hand when when you step up out of your home into the social life .

DISCLAIMER: Ye nahi bolungi ki merko hamesha ache ,sache dost mile - dogle , jhothe or matlabi log bhi mile ,par duniya k iss jungle mein kuch pak rooh rakhne wale , saath dene wale or samajhne wale bhhi mile or vo bohot Kam hn par azaaz hn . Issliye jab bhi m kahu dost , it means people you have a lot of memories with ,you share your mental and emotional status with ,you are not afraid of being judged , you don't only know each other's problems but insignificant and nervous types of things ,who may roast you ;laugh at you but don't let anyone else do that .And there is no comparison between friends and family .Both are special and I feel myself lucky to possess both .

Now I will state some real life instances just to show different reactions of friends and family in the same situation. Dost tumhara failaya hua rayta samette hain or Ghar wale tumhare failaye hue raste mein tumhe ghasitte hain.

Zara sa doston k saath khush hone ki koshish karo ,Ghar wale choice rakh dete hain ...hum ya vo kal k aaye dost or ek dost hn jo tumhari ya unki hi family se kitne hi hurt hon phir bhi tumhe yahi samjhate hn ki family first...family se badh k koi nahi .

Family can't digest friends and adjust with us spending time with them (or wasting time as they say it). Ghar wale bolte hain kuch bhi problem ho hamare saath share kiya karr ,hum solve kar denge...'teri galti nahi honi chahiye is silent' kyuki agar tumhari galti nikli toh unki reputation kharab ho jayegi par dost bolte nahi hain ,jab bhi koi bhi problem ho jee jaan laga dete hain solve karne k liye or jatate bhi nahin .

I am sure you do not wake up your family at 2AM or 3AM when someone or something is troubling you (either you overthink or you call your closest friend. If you are stuck somewhere ,you ask your friends and not family only to avoid all those stupid questions and judgements which may add to your problems.

True friends are the most under rated and undermined part of life ...you don't even get to count how many times they make you smile or efforts (untalked about) you make to stay with each - other .You tell your achievements first to your family but your battles ,failures and faults are more known to friends. They don't claim any rights and just go on with their responsibilities. Friendship is a kind of permanent relation ...once a friend is never a stranger again. Its not like friendship doesn't need time, care and attention but friends don't present it as demands rather as requirement and they don't even ask for it. I believe friendship is the simplest of all bonds and reduces complexities of all other bonds; makes social life and personal life easier, it forms a passage to cover the distance in these two life areas as per the circumstances. And you don't even make much efforts and still they are there standing by you .But it will be sin to take them for granted - chewing up your ego ,swallowing misunderstandings and forgetting some angrily said statements which were not meant literally and uttered in flow is the key to a healthy friendship .

My type of friendship is....I think a thousand times before calling someone as my friends but once I do, they will see the most clumpsy ,adventurous ,craziest and stupid side of me .I won't let anyone speak ill about them ,I'll justify them , I'll be honest with them but a bit irritated too .

And my friends do get irritated but once if I tell them ' I need you guys ',they will try out every possible method to fulfil that need. And I must say - I am very lucky when it comes to having friends. But there is a negative thing about me on the account of my overthinking. Sometimes ,I feel the friendship I put on such a high pedestal ,the friends I feel so proud to have - I don't matter to them . I think is it only me who is worried about this friendship ...a feeling of one - sidedness when my things are not reciprocated the way I want but I have been proven wrong everytime .It is just my pessimism that leads me to see a baseless side of situations. Little things which are actually little affect me a lot and I tense myself unnecessarily but unfortunately, my friends have to settle with this weirdness.

Also, log perfect nahi hote hain par kuch log rishton ko perfect banane ki koshish karte hain apni imperfections se . No one is perfect but relation can be made perfect if one has a pure heart and strong feelings of oneness.

The best part about having friends is you can complain to them about them itself. You need no filters. You can simply say- "I got hurt because of this statement of yours " or "let's clear misunderstandings ". Its not that you never get hurt by your friends but you must know it was not intentional or your friend was just disturbed and he let the catharsis on you and you understand him to the level you don't cry about it rather you tell let him know later ki tune jyada bol dia tha usne . This is much mature and beautiful than tune meri bejatti kardi or tune aisa kaise bol dia and then leave him .Your friend for sure will regret about it later but won't say a sorry or thank you and next time when you are not in your mind ,he will hear your frustration. That's the gesture of friendship . They don't say or show ,they do and don't let it come up .

Out of many myths and stereotypes that form the belief system of our families - one is - dost bigaad dete hn, galat cheezon mein dhakel dete hn, fanswa dete hn padhayi se dhyan bhataka dete hn . Everyone must have been a victim to this. But in reality real friendship saves you from falling into a bad company into a bad company or a toxic relationship . Kabhi tumhe vo nahi karne dete jisme tumhara nuksaan ho .And there is a practical difference- when family restricts you, their righteousness is mostly shaped by Is this socially correct ? But when friends deny something that is morally incorrect .Or tumhe kuch bhi samjhane k liye vo tumhe judge nahi karte yaa kiye ehsaan nahi jatate ,they simply bow down to a depth and they may fight with you ,abuse you but kuch bhi karke kuch galat nahi karne nahi denge . Our family doesn't know ki career k raaste mein ham kitni baar girte hain or phir kaise sambhalte hain ,ye sirf dost jante hn .Tum uske saath kitne plans banake destroy kar dete ho ,ye sirf dost jaante hain .Dost gali deke hi sahi ,career ko important karwa hi dete hn or ajeeb tareeke se motivate karte hn.

Then about having a life partner and related dimensions ... I don't know much...I am pretty unexperienced when it comes to relationship , but I know that much ...it creates an attention competition among friendship and relationship .What all I know is relationship has to be even ,maintained regularly, needs expressions and justifications is quite composite ,depends on a number of factors (show off too) and may break off if your standards are not met but friendship as I said ,is ever lasting.

No jealousy, no matter if you have known of each- other's existence for years but then somehow you come to know of your friend needing you and you'll bury entire past argument and come over which is rare in relationship where I don't know if the relation is permanent once made but the break up is forever after a relationship...then no comparison or soft corner can make you go back to him or her .

After analysing friendship from almost all the sides I put it forward to choose your friends really wisely .Good friends make your self adolescence but bad and toxic friends destroy your adulthood. The disadvantages and dark side of a false friendship are deadly and horrible .So ,it's okay if you don't have many friends or if you take time to make friends or even if you don't have any friend now . It is better to stay hungry and wait for food ,than to consume poison .Don't prove your parents right by domesticating snakes .

After friends and family ,we are all got to be part of social life - meaning "known strangers " - the one about whose tongue your family is so afraid of in, in whose mind your family wants to create a image and reputation- the "log" in "log kya kahenge". There is no social life as such just people making their lives , their rules and standards like other people want them to be .The problem comes up when this community (without any positive effect) expects us to be blindly in line with the customs ,traditions and limits they have set for you. Simply stupid and irrational rules. The rules which limit our fun, enthusiasm and youth and not necessary for discipline and morality - but to indirectly teach us adjustment I mean , bohot umar padi hh adjust karne k liye or adaptability seekhne k liye ,ye vo umar nahi hh. Bahar ghumna ,bike chalana, party karna ,love marriage karna ,apni marzi k kapde pehan na ,jisne chaho unse dosti karna - teens or twenties mein nahi karenge toh kab karenge ? These all form a list of MY CHOICES .

Aren't these things too personal for a society to form a code of conduct ?

Like who gave them the authority to decide on my behalf to set my limits ?

In India ,there is a term 'CHARACTERLESS ' and being termed that way is worse than dying .

And characterless kehlane k liye apko 3-4 relationships nahin rakhne hn...balki apko sirf apni zindagi apne hisab se ,apni sharton pe jeene ki hasrat Karni h and then you'll be labelled as worthy of worst treatment simply by wearing your favourite short skirts ,having a night duty (like in customer care or publishing journals) ,befriending boys (you feel comfortable with) ,laughing in street ,choosing a non conventional career in music or dance ,expecting your husband to respect you in front of everyone ,answering back in the same tone you have been questioned ,deciding to have a mutual divorce or asking for your property share as a daughter . (Well ,this is from my experience- things I have faced ,seen or heard in my hometown. Situation may differ on many grounds .)

You know , agar ladka bike seekhte hue gir jaye toh bolenge ...koi baat nahi ...girte padte hi seekhte hn...uth ja lekin agar ladki gir jaye toh #papa ki pari ...jab chalani nahi aati toh chalati kyu ho .

Agar ladka sharab peeye toh thoda daatenge ,sunayenge or kahenge ...jawani mein itna toh bacha bigadta hi hh or ladki agar iss bare m baat bhi kare toh worthy to be raped.

Agar ladka u chi Awaaz m baat kare toh usse ek thappad padega or dada- dadi Papa ko ye samjhayenge ki garam khoon h ,isse aram se baat kiya karr varna ye kuch kar baithega or ladki kare toh vahi ghar wale kahenge ki idhar aise bol rahi hh ,agle ghar jake naak katayegi .

India mein ladkiyon ko yahi soch k pala jata hh ki tumhari zindagi ka goal h - kisi ka ghar basana hh - uske liye tumhe sunni pade ,zillat sehni pade , khud k upar jitna marji compromise karna pade toh tum karogi ...tabhi Ghar baste hain. Kyuki tum insaan thodi ho - kabhi khoon k rishton k kabhi zimmedariyon ki. Tumhari puri zindagi challi jati h par hisab nahi hota tumhare paas ki sabki sunte sunte kaise chali gyi ...

Making compromise for family is commendable and should be but compromising yourself as an individual entity and making your self-respect adjust against everyone and everytime because only you are expected to care about your relation is not marriage or family service...its slavery.

And the worst thing about this concept of society is that our families are blind to it .Just because koi custom saalon se hota aa raha h ya just because sab karte hain,it doesn't become logical .Like Ghar walon k liye doesn't matter aap sahi ho ya galat ,khush ho ya gum mein ... what matters is vo char log jo kahi matter bhi nahi karte vo kya bolenge .But just think about this - jyada se jyada kya hi bolenge ...hum unke muh band nahi kar sakte par apne kaano mein toh rui daal sakte hain .

We are humans not a wall everyone in society trying to paint in their own colour. Our families are careful about our perception in society because they are careless in passing comments about other's children. Hamen Ghar walo ne samajik ijjat ki murti bana dia h and people are free to weigh us against their conceptions . For example, agar kisi ki ladki apne lover k saath bhag jaye toh saare log parvarish pe ,uski azaadiyon pe , uske parents pe, sawal uthane lag jayenge lekin kisi ka husband usse mar raha ho toh vo personal matter ho jata h . Hypocrisy!!

If I describe the height of orthodoxy and depth to which it is entrenched in my land . I come from a place jaha agar kisi ko dusri ladki ho jaaye toh mattam manaya jaata h ,jab ladka paisa hota h toh badi celebration hoti h kyuki ladke future or hope represent karte hain , ladkiyon ko unke complexion ,breast size ,height or body shape pe 'fit for marriage' ya 'dahej jyada dena padega' mein categorise kiya jata h ,ladki ki ek ek second ka hisab rakha jata h, ghar se bahar tab bhehte hain jab bilkul zaroori ho or agar 5 minute bhi late ho jaye toh saare Ghar walo ko heart attack aane lagta h.

Apni beti or bete ko same school mein karwake Maa baap soch te hain humne ladki k upar ehsaan kar dia...like education agar mere bhai ka right h toh mere liye vo opportunity kyu h?

Shorts agar mera bhai pehan raha h toh garmi lag rahi hogi or agar m pehan rahi hu toh m attention invite kar rahi hu .

And I think this is not only a fact of my place but almost all rural areas and also urban areas upto some extent .

My social life has been adventurous because I am a liberal and radical at same time .I have always tried to convince by my logics and rationale. My friends understand me ,but my family tell me to keep quite if I don't have "social manners and maturity" , my teachers have always appreciated and have enlightened me with the struggles and troubles if I don't change and my neighbours about what they believe but I do.

And because of this "bravery " of being myself and choosing rebelliousness ,I have been through many unpleasant experiences but this is nothing if I get a living heart ,I I don't need to eat my thoughts ,if I am able to face myself in mirror and answer to GOD ...

There is a difference- being wrong and different .

I HOLD MY OPINIONS ,I PRESENT THEM STRONGLY AND THEN ACT AS AN INDIVIDUAL.

Lost and busy friends
    "Jo hamare din se raat tak k waqt k tukde hua karte the
    Ab har guzarte pal k tukde mehsoos karwa rahe hain
    Jinke saath andhere ko bhi saja dia karte the
    Ab unke bina har rang apna libas chhod raha or hum bus dekhe
jaa rahe hain
    Jinki hansti hui haqeeqat na jaane kab yaadon ki faryad ban gyi
    Ab uss haqeeqat ko guzra arsa bol kar yaadon ko asra dene se
inkar kar rhe hn"

ᮬᮬᮬ

Life goes on...with or without friends
    "Zindagi h jana, koi kaid nahi
    Ki jo ek bar aa jaye vo hamesha vo milega vahi
    Dost toh aate jaate rehte hn ,kyuki sab ko
    Pohochna hota h kahin na kahin

Safar lamba h, hote hain kuch kadam jo thodi der saath chalte hain

Par unn kadmo ka apna makam hh ,raaste alag hone par hum kyu bhool jate hain

Thodi aage tak akele chalenge toh naye musafir mil jayenge or phir tumhare safar ko

tanha kar denge...ab chalo maan jate hain

Ye takleef ya shikayat ka masla nahi balki

Hansti khelti yaadon ko batorne ka moka hh

Manzil tak k safar m ye lazmi hh

Jo ek bar sakht kadmo se chal diye unhe aaj tak kiski judai ne roka hh"

᭢᭢᭢

"Tumhare galat hone pe jo bhale hi tumhara saath na de

Par tumhara saath chhode bhi na

Jo tumhari Jang mein beshaq samne adkar tumhe bachaye nahi

Par piche khada hokar tumhe shiqast kabool karne de bhi nahi "

᭢᭢᭢

"Jiske samne galti kabool sako

Jiske samne aaina dekh sako

Jiske samne ansuon ko ijazat de sako

Jiske samne apna aitbaar mehfooz rakh sako

Ek aisi rooh ,jiska shukriya Ada tum apni duaon mein bhi kar sako "

᭢᭢᭢

"I know you don't get me

But please don't leave me

If I do something not right, don't let me

I'll try to change ,you can bet me

᭢᭢᭢

I know we are not same
    But hear this, your going away is not a game
    Yes,we cross words but please never blame
    I'll fix it all ,my words are not lame
    I know I am not the one you wished for
    But I have never had someone like you before "

ᐳᐳᐳ

"Zabardasti ki zindagi ya
    Zabardast zindagi
    Koi ek chhuno
    Doglepan Ki duniyadari ya
    Apne aap se ehsaas ki yaari
    Par ho toh issi duniya se
    Tum dono m jee loge
    Chhodo rehne do"

ᐳᐳᐳ

"Jab khayal-e-zamana sun ke
    Kisiki khwaishen khudkushi karti hn
    Toh kon kispe tohmat lagane k kabil bachta hh
    Vaha Khuda k banaye ye insaan or insaaniyat
    Dono har jati hn"

ᐳᐳᐳ

"Apne mujhse Lambi zindagi jee hh
    Kayi manzar dekhe honge
    Par tajurbe ki sarad k bajay
    Baharon m fiza aati hh
    Kayi mausam dekhe hn
    Itna toh jante hi honge"

- Sikanda

SEVEN
CAREER AND BALANCE

You know, Why I believe life of teenagers is difficult? The reason being in age when mind wants fun and enjoyment ,career is also a requirement- wanting to be cool and focused at the same time - wanting restrictions and liberty at the same time - understanding the criticality of youth on which our future depends as well as the feeling that we craved for this energy since childhood - wanting to socialise but qualitatively as you are also afraid getting stuck in situations where there is no way out - learning to hide many things from family to trusting deeply and for some ,finding a partner too. All this creates loads of pressure on our heart and mind and adolescents end up in neither having an adventurous youth nor making it a great career. There steps in the balance of life- which is the toughest part and in the end kuch na kuch chhut hi jata h .

So, I have come out with an explanation from my experiences. There are four institutions of life like its pillars and even without one of them ,your life doesn't have a meaning and I assign equal importance to all of them imagining life as a car with four tyres and one punctured tyre can hinder the entire journey .

First is YOU - your views ,your opinions your choices and your decisions signifying how much you mean to yourself and how much you respect yourself in the way you present or take a stand on certain incidences and it makes you feel having a strong back bone .Self - care is an important facet of this .Decision making and analysing all pros and cons and weighing up all consequences and then reaching to a conclusion is a sort of personal development and leads to mental growth .

Then is FAMILY - your blood relations .You are just a human with them but you are a son/daughter ,a sibling ,a cousin ,a grandchild , a nephew and a niece .They bring you up in a better way than their salaries could afford ,making best things available to you and giving you a heart filled with memories and other emotions. There is no point of breathing if you don't have attachments of love,care , compassion building in your heart since childhood and your parents have got a connection with you before you knew them or before you knew anything in this world (not even you name). They make tough efforts to make you sincere about your career and keep a check on distractions you may have (though they sometimes turn toxic too)

Next comes ,career - you need to consider that your family won't always be there with you and at a point of time you'll be required to having your own family whose daily requirements will be your call ..Also ,you can't depend on your parents' income after your education is done and you become employable and you'll need to have money earned on your own with your efforts and achievements. For that career ,you have to make up your mind and start early ,may be in secondary school itself and then manage school life or college life ...academics with extra curricular activities or tours and hanging out with friends . Career means a secure future in whichever field you can or you want to . In current Era, there are lots of choices and options available to students and by various means in different sectors. Apart from going for govt jobs ,you can also find significant earning by making reels on social media ,be a comedian or motivational speaker , be a poet or author a book ,be a model , be a gym trainer ,a script writer whatever you choose if you have required skill and innate talent

The last one is your friends- your only comfort ,your age mates ,you relate with them most and they understand you ,listen to your non sense life plays .I've expressed the most I could in former pages about this institution of friendship...The basis of social life and height of personal life ...or may be, a bridge between two .

So , these four things frame your life in a picture with four corners and each corner being spiky. You can't live without any one of these . And balancing them is biggest question as well as biggest answer of life .Sometimes, you must fall in dilemmas : only if I discuss about the situations I had to cope up...Compromising on ME because my family didn't appreciate my self respect and career would flee from my hands if I paid too much attention on what I thought. No one agrees to my principles and career I have decided for myself needs patience, acceptance and tolerance. Or compromising on friends because they are just considered time pass ,no significant time should be given to them .And the worst one was when I was asked to follow a career my family chose for me and this was the exosphere of intermixing of elements when I decided to keep them all separate and thus satisfied - like fighting for my career violently outside home but justifying peacefully inside the doors or like not telling family about my friends' secrets and also about how I am enjoying my life with them not allowing any flow of information between friends and family or dividing my day after studying to talk to my buddies and spend a fraction of it with my family. I learnt this very late. Only minimum interaction should be there when by no means it can be avoided and assigning each one of them their own arena and going with my day schedule according. Otherwise ,I still recall a time when I almost messed up everything on the account of immaturity of taking life as a whole.

Then a very famous issue occurs - choose your career yourself according to your interests, capabilities, Intelligence Quotient (IQ) and Emotional quotient (EQ) taking a closed shot at your strengths and weaknesses and realistic and prudent approach towards the limit upto which you can push yourself and if you can actually imbibe all those qualities and capture all that knowledge in some specific amount of time and in an organised way,then go for it .

Otherwise, take as much time you need for self awareness you want to because its perfectly okay to be in 9th or 10th and not know which stream you are going to take .But once when you have decided , your own family may be against it if it's not conventional or if it does sound socially cool like many of your cousins or your sibling or neighbours or your family 's aqaintances and you will have to take a firm stand there ...afterall it's about your future and no one else can set limits for you , no one knows you more than yourself .For your family ,it's only about comments and reactions of people around ;,but for you ,it's a question which will decide every second after your today . So...fight, argue ,disagree ,prove your points and try hardest to be permitted to pursue with near perfection and a perfect opportunity for you .

At the end of the day ,doing what you love hits different than forcibly loving or adjusting what you are made to do .

Career is all about a game of yesterday, today and tomorrow...climbing stairs ,each moment,you know! Coming out of yesterday's zone to make a happier and more productive today and then taking both yesterday and today with mistakes and pressure to be put on tomorrow and presenting it as yesterday on today. Isn't it confusing?

It simply means we drag things, sometimes ,unnecessarily and forget to forget yesterday, to live today and leave tomorrow for time when it will become today. Remember, every today will become a yesterday and every tomorrow brings with itself remnants of today .

So, why you restrict yourself from living this day?

Why don't you divide your day between now and next ?

Why do you leave opportunities to do something memorable in the moment you are breathing so that instead of burdening future ,you little enlighten and stay calm today?

Why didn't you go to that birthday party - that person was your close friend, you hurt him on your special day ?

Why did you not join your classmates in that trip - you could collect a bouque of memories to thrive on forever ?

Why did you not participate in that dance performance or for that speech - you could have learnt a lot what book don't teach ?

I, personally, don't appreciate daily parties, trips or functions- this dailyness or usuality makes all these events lose charm and these stop becoming special to you .But I affirm being an audience is worse than not so good participant.

Trust me,you won't lose at your academics - in fact, this all will help you provide a kind of recreation ,revival and energy. Its okay if you don't have money to present a gift to your friend at his birthday party ,just make a card of your own or some other craft material(handmade) .No problem if you can't afford a trip ,you can watch online videos or if possible, go to nearer place .No one will laugh at you if their expectations from performance are not met ,you learnt to step on stage audience could not .

Being a college student, aaj piche mud k dekhti hu toh lagta h kaash, ek do lecture or bunk mar kar kisi Khali room m gappe mar liye hote ,ek do rules or todke maze liye hote ,jinhe class mein nahin jante thhe unka tiffin bhi khol k kha lia hota ,teachers ki personal life mein thoda or interest liya hota ,self study k liye kaash vo games ka lecture na gawaya hota function m dance ya music m participate kiya hota , kabhi juniors se bhi panga leke dekh lia hota ya doston se itna door ho jayenge ye pehle pata hota .

Aaj mujhe dhang se yaad bhi nahi ki kitne marks score kiye the yaa kitne ghante padhayi karti thi ,par ye ache se yaad h ki kitni daant padi ,class m kiski ladai hui ,kon kiske saath committed h , test m kitni cheating ki ,unse baat karne k liye kitna struggle kiya or school mein m kitni famous thi . Isn't it all interesting .

Yes ,future is important but so is today ,that too equally. Like if I bunked lectures ,I'll take notes from someone or help from you tube or teachers ; if I broke rules and got caught ,I'll say sorry ; or if there is a fight in class - I'll beat or get beaten but without any later grudges .All those yesterdays were also an unpredictable future for me but my today is leaving happily in memorising it .

My point is to solve the puzzle of unarranged pieces of improperly shaped objects in life game .Its all about fitting your yesterday ,today and tomorrow in a sense of continuity and a more specific term TIME MANAGEMENT .Scrapping out time for listening music at least 30 minutes a day ,gossiping with your friends online for an hour or at least going to meet them, 5 minutes for medication ,some two hours for online activity (watching reels or web series) ,and a complete rest on Sunday for leisure - I think isn't much for living in today .Even this light schedule can help you study effectively and efficiently for 6-7 hours .Time table is a good way of ensuring that .My time tables don't include what I'll include what I'll do in which hour of the day . I am flexibe about timings but serious about that fixed amount of work that I have got to complete
.

Another markable point is the continous conflict between mind and heart .Mind doesn't feel and heart doesn't think. Mind is opaque to emotional upheavals and reactions when heart is sometimes opaque to explanation, logic and reason .Mind is something over which you can exercise 100 per cent control but there is always a part of heart which will never be under your understanding and always be a mystery for you. It is easy to change your mind but it is damn difficult to make your heart understand about possible consequences and problems which may arise . My teacher tells me you achieve half success if you are able to develop a subordination amongst heart and mind .Blindly following any one of them is injurious to your career health and life .Learning to master mind and having an understanding heart is the art of survival. You can't imagine any situation of your life being averted unilaterally.

And my teacher also tells me - if at any point you are confused about what you should do and you are not getting a thing and when your heart and mind are fighting and all attempts to holistic solutions have failed - Go with your heart. Your heart is never wrong . Heart is bold ,brave and strong and you need guts to match actions with your heart. I also believe GOD resides in heart and HE can't suggest anything toxic .The deadliest combination ever on this earth is an emotional heart and smart heart. You are unstoppable unfathomable and unraveling if you can achieve this. Nothing is outside your limits then.So, trust your heart for actions and listen to your mind for reactions and then decide collectively the best possible way out .

After knowing the length and breadth of career ,let's switch to its depth - MOTIVATION: the food of your career , the source of your success and hope of betterment of present conditions .Easy to discuss ,tough to actually feel all thoughts of strength ,determination and Self- control. A motivation is having an image of a moment in your mind when you are in that attire ,exercising all those rights and responsibilities you dreamt of since you decided to go for thus ,reminding yourself of anxieties you had ,failures you recovered and setbacks you recieved - the struggle that was unleashed on you by your dream .That very particular image makes you forget all discouragement and be hard at your hardwork ,instill a feeling in you - you can make that dream image characters move with investment of sweat ,possibilities to come up ,opportunities to appear and all those motivational quotes or examples you heard of thought to be applied .

Motivation is like a flower which blossoms all flowers .you find nothing impossible then. Having an image of you being successful should act as an incentive not that you dwell in imagination 24×7 and forget reality or that you trust your image so much that it turns into obsession .An ideal situation or a utopia should be the near perfect target but not considering the possibility of foolishness on your part . Fate is also a factor and fate is not always in favour. Keep that sky into your mind but don't forget the distance between sky and soil . Failure is a fact and has many factors not necessirily lack of your seriousness or sincerity. Accepting failures as now low priced stone but later as valuable pearl to be decorated on frame of success is crucial . You can't achieve success by not considering failures and just dreaming of success .Its rude but real that you can't ignore a possibility that you can fail too and success is not your only fortune .Otherwise ,this ignorance leads to murder of hope ,patience ,self confidence and SELF too. You don't remain the same person or you don't remain even(in case of suicides). Har baar hum jo chahte hn vo nahin ho sakta. Many times ,things will be unpredictable and unexpected and can go against your thought. And I agree , when you lose at something ,everything breaks inside you - all those promises you made to yourself, all that fun you planned after result ,all those dreams and expectations you expected yourself to accomplish ,all that time you devoted ,the success you had wished for and your worship seem to be drawn deep and this all takes you along. May be the moments surge further but you are stuck there . That condition is understandable immediately after your failure is informed ,what is abnormal is that condition persists and become a part of your life .May be you accepted the failure but still don't find yourself able to muster up courage to face tomorrow now .You dwell in your yesterday, waste today and lose tomorrow .And in order to catch up or drive away from reality or may develop an addiction to mobile phone ,binge eating ,binge watching, becoming an atheist or drugs even. Stay away from being habitual to anything that has no end . After some 4 or 5 years of failing ,these moments may not matter to you ot may you realised you reached better place .And you will be okay with fate then - you will develop an understanding, keep going ,burying failures and stepping ahead are assets of life .Don't miss out at them . Keep alive in yourself the flame of motivation - you don't need someone's lecture to tell you what you have to have and how you are going to get that .

Standing up again ,rebuilding your mind ,re establishing remnants of heart makes you worthy of future success .Respecting the unexpectedness of life - no matter how hard you did plan or work is the only way to protect yourself from falling a victim to failure. Don't let anything break that flow if internal Motivation within you. Explore more opportunities, careers and options and refix your goals while redesigning your revolutions .

Kuch na kuch toh Khuda ne tumhare naseeb mein bhi chhod rakha hoga

Tumhe likhte waqt vo tumhare khilaf nahi raha hoga !

Aaj phir mehnat k patthron ko bejaan ghans k beech takrane ki chahat aayi hh

Aaj bujha di thi ab phir se thand aayi h

Thandi hawayon m nayi aag ko lapetne ki taqat aayi h

Par bhaga dia hawa ko ,bezubaan ghans ne aise guhaar lagayi hh

Jag gye rang-e-zameen ,dhuen ne asmaan tak aisi khabar pohochayi hh

ᖰᖰᖰ

"Kal, Kyu or kaash karte karte

Kuch bhi haath nahi laga

Toh chal pade,

Thokar khayi, gire ,sambhale,

Rude,uthe ,phir chal pade

Issliye kuch na milne pe bhi

Bura nahi laga"

ᖰᖰᖰ

FUTURE

Something not included in sand of our hand ,we can only expect

The most curious question whose reply is upon how your present react

Tomorrow is a puzzle, that would vanish if you make it today perfect

It may be as unpredictable as the weather without any use of what you suspect

It's not a different page if your life rather a length of remarks on same page ,it's something not direct

Because pages don't turn as the day passes ,they turn for bright when you look at life from different prospect

Don't waste this precious breadth to know blur the bronchi would be ,derive energy and remove this defect

Free yourself from this prison of anxiety and stress and secure your future by signing this pact

Stay forward on your tracts ,keep forward your steps and make each step a success and success a fact

Success is not 'I will',it's based on what you will at this very moment, it's just about what you select

In this strive for future now ,don't accept just approximate and don't forget a fair retrospect

Future is the biggest query lurking on our existence with unknown effect

But when we know the way, we would trek it and so replies would be indirect

See it through water you are now in ,your aspirations would become achievements in this aspect

Uncertainties are the suspense of life ,trigger of today and about activeness you collect!!

ᐁᐁᐁ

"Kahan guzre Kal ki baat karte ho

Yaha toh aane wala kal aaj ka picha nahi chhodta

Ae insaan tu kal ki fikr or faryad

Apne mukaddar or Karam pe kyu chhodta"

᯼᯼᯼

"Daftar ka har khat chhan mara
   Par paigam-e-manzil nahi mila
   Phir dakiya dikha mujhe
   Jisne pohochaya tha har panne ko uske anjaam tak
   Isse pata chala mujhe ki mere panne ka intezar
   Meri manzil pe ho raha h
   Bss der h toh vahan pohochne tak"

᯼᯼᯼

HEART VS MIND
   "Jang -e- Zindagi mein aksar amne samne hoti hain do fauj - dil
or dimag
   Jeet ta koi nahi h par ye Jang jeene nahi deti
   Par m ye tark rakhti hu ki dimag ped ki vo tehni h jo Zara si hawa
ki or chal deti hh
   Or dil vo jadd se ukkhad jayegi lekin mitti m qayam rehti hh"

᯼᯼᯼

" Nahi waqif hu apne kal se
   Par khofzada hu agle pal se
   Nahi aitmaad mujhe mukaddar par
   Manzil meri Zidd se beshaq vhi h par
   Aksar raste or thokar ki alag shaklien hoti hn
   Gum jaane m or gir Jane m shiqast mehsoos hoti h"

᯼᯼᯼

"Mujhe fiza nahi apni marzi chahiye
   Agar kaid mera mukaddar h toh mujhe maut chahiye
   Apna tajurba chahti hu ,mujhe khud ki kahani chahiye
   Ek ek sabak stare ki tarah apne kirdar pe lagana chahti hu
   Mujhe meri apni zindagi chahiye"

᯼᯼᯼

• 68 •

"Honsle har fikr ko fariq kar dete hain
    Bss udaan-e-manzil na milne m qayamat si lagti hh
    Zameen pe saari azaishen mile to bhi
    Asmaan ka vo ek tukda ekhtiyar m chahiye
    Meri rooh aise zidd rakhti hh"

- Sikanda

EIGHT

DARK AND DEEP DEPRESSION

My intuition says I won't be able to say much about this but trust me, this is the emotion I've experienced most. Let me clear this that it is not a joke or relatable meme trending on social media - it is much more consuming ,killing , and destroying in it's nature and only those who have seen the sword in their hands dripping with their heart' s blood know how horrible it is.

Let me clear a misunderstanding - sadness and depression are totally different - just like a cloudy day and a moonless night differ from each other .Sadness is a emotion depression is a persistent state of mind .Sadness is a mood and very temporary, depression removes all other moods. Sadness is normal while depression takes away all normality .Sadness is downward jump from peak to another level of slope but depression is steep ,right down into valley of darkness .Sadness allows tears .Depression disregards the importance of tears .Sadness is like eyes closed and depression is similar to being blind. Sadness is when you are too disturbed and all your to be happy have failed but depression is when you stop searching happiness and nothing can distract you to make you alive in true sense - you accept everything .Those who are in depression never say it rather they see this is as a recovery time or they are having "maturity" by not being excited about anything. Sadness demands that things go your way ,depression doesn't demand .Depression is a barren land of burried trust ,expectations, relations and memories .And I must say sadness ought to be respected and depression ought to be ousted.

Sadness is very normal. Little things cause it .When you are sad ,you don't say it to anyone, you aren't frustrated but you are worried - a lot of things are coming in your mind and your happy mood is ruined .You don't feel anything happening . And sadness is weathery.

Kabhi choti choti baaton pe bhi dil udaas hota h

Or kabhi kabhi khushi itni jyada hoti hh ki badi se badi baat ko bhi jaane deta h!!

Or insaan ek bar dukhi ho jaye toh rone k liye bahane bante hn

Vo tamaan manzar jab isse pehle jitni bar bhi roye ho !!

Tum har waqt hans toh nahi sakte toh kya masla h agar kabhi phoot k roo liye toh ... vo bhi zaroori hh,

Ehsaaso ki mehfil gam k bina adhuri hh!

Jab dukhi hote ho toh tanhayi pasand karte hn - kisi se kuch nahi kehna, kisi pe ilzaam nahi lagana ,khud ki galtiyan yaad aane lagti hn or sirf khud se sikhayat karne ki zaroorat lagti hh.

Thodi der baad sab theek ho jayega - haqeeqat dheere dheere haqeeqat tumhare andar utarne lagegi, halat hazam hone lagenge or tum 'behtar ho sakta tha' ya ' jo soch rakha tha' isse bahar aa jaoge.

For example - you go to a party and your favourite cousin doesn't show up; your friend couldn't come out of some emergency when you were waiting for him at the place ;your favourite pencil, geometry box ,hankerchief or one of your good dresses gets lost somewhere and you are unable to find its replace or the replace can't replace the thing you were emotionally attached with ; you prepared hard this time for exams but ended up scoring much less below your expectations; you had a fight with someone and it was totally his fault but both of you had to get punished or you hurt someone unintentionally, someone close to you.

These are the things you can't blame anyone except fate and neither can you complain to anyone except GOD (who else will listen) .After the immediary period is over, you start looking for alternatives or get okay with whatever had happened. Sadness isn't a fault .Gum ko galti manna bhi ek galti hh .Let the air melancholy come with you and then let it go with flow - afterall this air has also got a route .

Depression is climatic . Going in depression is not mere disappointment from current incidences rather it is pushing yourself to an isolated cell ,and then you locked it from inside and then thrown the keys don't know where. There is hardly any way out because no one knows of your existence in that cell and you keep dying alone there unless your mental state experiences a total shock and you realise the life in life or unless GOD instructs someone to find keys and open it up. Depression comes from a trauma and trauma is when an incidence you get sad about repeats itself again and again in every situation and you find no solution than crying ,complaining- you start turning neutral and not normal ... now the incidence doesn't matter in you...no affect in your mood but your entire attitude towards life begins to change for you if such incidences increase in influence and number .Way to depression is staring down when you let yourself be thrown from one stair to another in as life flows (each stair is very heighted). Like after your cousin doesn't come in wedding - other family functions and events also become pale for an account of one or the other reasons .So, you stop attending weddings . Or when all of your friends start getting busier in their lives and you now find it hard to make new friends and even getting a work for you. So, you stop hanging out even with your old friends even when you get a chance .You start developing chagrin in your heart for people you have always lived with and you are not able to analyse any positive or negative change in your behaviour .Your favourite objects now do not matter to you and you stop being stubborn to look for that particular and your favourite thing - like you accept everything now without any complain . During exams, you have been pressing yourself hard for concentrated efforts with persistence and perseverance but results are not in line with your hardwork in every exam .So, now you feel futile ,worthless and stop doing any mental labour .Sadness becomes your comfort zone or from a mood it now marks your behavioural pattern .In depression ,you don't feel anything .Isolation and fear of people is first concrete step . Staying alone can be a choice but depression makes it your necessity . You get scared of people's questions about your dissappearances .You feel nobody loves you, cares about you or is really concerned about your mental health. You start avoiding social gatherings and friends or trying to make your life better.

In depression ,

Pehle ek ek din mushkil hota hh

Phir din kaise kat rahe hn ye pata hi nahi hota hh

Depression makes you take back all the trust you ever adored your relations with ,all the expectations from family, friends, you yourself or even GOD . You don't become hard or mature rather you become emotionless and either you become emotionless and either you start screaming over petty things ...your temperament becomes violent . You don't care about anything else or anyone out there . Or become all silent .You don't feel anger or resentment but still shout unintentionally not knowing you are hurting your closed ones. Your shout isn't meant to invite attention or making people care about you but it becomes kind of uncontrollable and unpredictable part of behavior. And no knows that those screams are coming from a heart which is living in tense air and burried hope i.e. its all silent inside and violent outside .Only you know how tough this survival gets for you .In nights ,when you earlier used to appreciate used to appreciate beauty of skies ,moons and stars . Instead ,now you close your windows .And you go to sleep but sleep doesn't welcome you and that's why you are afraid of nights .Nights turn irritating though you love dark but you find no peace in it. You know what it means to have an exerted body and a depressed heart. - like in your attempt to sleep you keep looking at walls and ceiling of your room with just regretting how stupid you used to be but you feel no proud at your disillusionment too. You barely sleep for 3-4 hours and waste 2-3 hours daily to get sleep.

Sleep becomes a physical requirement and not a mental need .Your physical health also start worsening . Either your remind yourself of all the pains and struggles you have gone through everytime you are not surrounded by some time or you start forgetting everything your memory no longer helps you. What all you remember is what you are ? and not 'what you used to be ' Your dynamic personality fades away ,your confidence gets burried deeper than your trust and expectations plus patience doesn't mean anything to you. You become a totally different person - you being labelled as egoistic ,one with negative attitude ,insensitive , rude and bitter...all this becomes normal to you and you don't find it important to explain or justify it to anyone.

Not only from gradually stairing down , depression can come from a shock too - like death of your closed one ,betrayal by best friend, abandonment by your girlfriend or boyfriend, family problems (seeing your parents violently fighting) . In depression you absorb the shock but snatch the pain you received to tie tightly in the shackles of heart . That pain, that suffering keeps you reminding of how unfair life has been with you . You break all bonds with yourself - you no longer worry about career ,family or friends .

Moving on is not known to you because you still dwell on memories . Moving on isn't forgetting past rather accepting past as past ,recognising the time distance present and past and respecting that distance .Moving on is tough but it helps you answer the calls of your future marked in present. Moving on is maturity and I have already stated depression is not maturity .

Not having many expectations but possessing patience and hope is maturity . Not blind trust or not trusting everyone but faith in GOD is maturity

. Knowing the evil intentions of some people around you and avoiding them but changing yourself for yourself and for people is maturity

. Not opening up with everyone but choosing wisely and sharing everything with at least one or two people is maturity .

Maturity changes your attitude not your entire personality. Being immature atleast in front of at least one person is maturity.

Depression with itself insomnia ,stress, anxiety ,overthinking and helplessness .. It isn't easy. And the peak of depression is you faking out entire existence- you smiling so that nobody questions you or judges as weak . Your day is shared with others though you don't want to and you keep looking for escapes during day but there is no one to save your from yourself at nights when you do crave for company but don't ask for it. Nights better know how insensitive you are to yourself- your impatience ,restlessness- only the dark air of your room is aware of it. No one in this world ,no one in this life absolutely no one - Not even GOD , you think, find you deserving enough to make you a part of it . This world and this life does sound appear of your own. You regard yourself as a fault of GOD .

Depression is devastation - a murder of childhood , adolescence and adulthood - all in one go .You learn fakeness ,distrust and show off being unaware of the fact you are hurting people close to you who love you.

My experience of depression ate a part of me from within and maybe , even if I am out of it now , I won't be able to bring that innocence, that girl who lived in this flesh . That girl who easily forgot unpleasant incidence ,who cared about everyone and who preserved her ties as her pearls but the girl who is writing this doesn't care ,has learnt to be selfish and has developed trust issues and forgotten her anger issues .I don't know if this is maturity but I crave for my old me. Even if you somehow get out of depression ,you aren't healed ,you have just accepted the hurt.

While the peak of depression is fake smile ,the depth of depression is wishing for death deep inside . You want to end your life because many things in your life didn't go as per your way . You don't want sympathy, don't want to be loved ,don't want circumstances to change ,you just have to escape and death is a permanent escape . You think your entire life will go planning and crying . So instead of wasting it you feel to live , would be more struggling, troubling ,terrifying and horrible and death is better. But trust me ,jis din zameen pe tumhara maqsad khatam ho jayega ,Khuda bula lega .Vo tumhare haal se waqif hh.

Agar usne tumhe abhi tak zinda rakha hh

Toh yakeenan tumhare naseeb m kuch behtar likha hh

Abhi honsla kho gaya h toh taqat bankar tumhare paas wapas bhi aayega . Sabr rakho. Agar har rishte se thak kar ,zindagi ko bojh samjh rahe ho toh ,kuch waqt baad shayad rishte na ho or zindagi bhi na ho. Toh JIYO! jeene k bahane dhundo ,jeene ka tareeka badal lo par jeena mat chhodo ....

kisi insaan ya apne liye na sahi

Khuda k liye hi sahi

And mind it - having trust issues and flexing it isn't maturity and isn't cool either .Everyone is fighting his own battles and continuing it till GOD asks you to is your responsibility. Losing hope is a sin ,forgetting your faith is a sin and stop making wishes to GOD ; not expecting from him is a sin .

Jab zindagi se thhak jao toh sab kuch khuda pe chhod do ,apni Zindagi ka Khuda bankar isse khatam mat KaroAgar tumhe iss zindagi se nawaza gaya h toh kuch farz hain tumhare , kuch ummedien hn Khuda ko tumse or bohot saari zimmedariyan hh jinhe pura karna h abhi unke liye jo tumhara zikr apni duaon mein karte hain . Zindagi agar kabhi zamane k samne mazak ban bhi jaye toh apni jaan lekar tum iska mazak mat udao .

Apna tajurba bayan kar rahi hu : zindagi behad mushkil hh , bohot aziyat hoti h zabardasti zinda rehne mein , insaan ko dobara apne aitbar ko khada karne m - vo bikhar jata h , Roshni ki zaroorat hoti h par insaan uski talash nahi karta but

" YE WAQT BHI BEET JATA HH

SAB SAMBHAL JATA HH"

This is what depression feels like :

Samajh hi nahi aata kisi se kya baat karu m

Baaton ka pitara shayad khali ho gaya h ,issliye thodi chup chap rehne lagi hu m

Na narazgi h ,na shikayat or na ana hh phir bhi sabse door hone lagi hu m

Dil m jo toofan thha vo aaj bhi barkarar h par ab apni khamoshi se jawab de rahi hu m

Iss tapdili ko maine nahi bulaya hh naa jane aisi kyu ho rahi hu m

"Alfaaz khatam nahi hue hn
  Sirf Awaaz band hui h
  Nazare khatam nahi hui h
  Sirf nazren jhuki hui hn
  Taqat khatam nahi hui h
  Sirf chahat Kam hui h
  Baarish khatam nahi hui h
  Bss abhi hawa ki baari aayi hui hh
  Zindagi khatam nahi hui hh
  Sirf iski vo zindadilli hi toh kahi kho gyi hh"

ᖰᖰᖰ

"Koi kehta h har dard k aansu mehfooz hn ankhon m
  Toh kisi ki ansuon se mulakat hoti h toh sirf andheron m"

৵৵৵

"Umeed bhi h or
   sabr bhi kar liya hh
   Khwaish bhi hh or
   khud ko Sambhal bhi liya hh
   Khuda se mili khushi bhi hh
   or zaroorat-e-zamana bhi haasil kar liya hh"

৵৵৵

"Andhi k baad sukoon ki saans aayi hh
   Jo udd gaya usse jane diya
   Jo kuch KHUDA ne mere paas chhod diya
   Ab usse sametne ki baari aayi h
   Jhoothi muskurahat ki koshish karne k pal gye
   Ab muskurake kal pe mehnat k pal ki baari ayi h"

৵৵৵

"Zindagi ne iss qadar sikhaya hh
   Ki ab samjhauta ghate ka sauda nahi lagta
   Ab khud ko khush karna galat nahi lagta
   Ab koi bhi waqt-e-sitam mushkil nahi lagta
   apne aap ko mukaddar k hawale chhod dene se ab darr nahi lagta"

৵৵৵

"Khud k khilaf khada hun
   Kuch samajh nahi aa raha h
   Har beetta pal mujhse faisla maang raha hh
   Naa maidan chhodna hh
   Naa hathiyar uthana hh
   Naa jeetna hh
   Naa Shaheed hona hh
   Shiqast toh meri hi hogi
   Phir bhi mujhe puri jang dekhni hh

KHUDA bhi sochta hoga
Iss pal k baad ise phir ek zindagi deni hh"

❧❧❧

POV : You blame GOD and think of suicide
    "Khuda ne itni pyaari duniya banayi
    Or iss duniya mein rehne walon ne
    Khuda ki hi galti batayi
    Haa nahi h asaan iss duniya m rehna
    Lekin kya tumhari guzri nasalon ne
    Pyaar se KHUDA k bharose
    Ibadat ki raah m
    Khushiyon ki chah m
    Khwabon ki naav m
    Or dil ki neki m
    Khuda ka shurkriya ada karne ki
    Rasam nahi banayi??"

- Sikanda

NINE
OPINIONS ABOUT ME

Readers , now I'll enlist opinions of some people really close to my heart and who have known me for more than a year. You may feel like they are hyping me but all I asked for was an honest picture they had in their mind of a 19 year old .

1. HINA MAM

She is my history teacher and she taught me from 9th to 12th.

After GOD, it is she who owns my trust. I feel like through her , GOD helped me live and heal. And she is the mom I found in teens .No one can understand me , can explain to me ,can listen to my daily dramas... the way she has done .

I could never have imagined myself authoring a book or writing shayaris ...without her .

Her positivity , her faith ,her smile is just so beautiful and strong.

I feel grateful to have her in life.

This is how she describes me:

"1. You are emotional and sensitive girl.

2. Rational minded

3. Have a liberal mindset.

4. You wanted to explore the world. 5

5. Ambitious girl

6. Lonely from inside .

7.While angry, you speak bluntly (speak things which should not be said)

8. You have to learn emotional balance (where to stay calm and where and how to react.

9.I COULD NEVER HAVE GONE INTO WRITING POEMS AND THEN SHAYARIS WITHOUT MY TEACHER...HER BEING THERE .

10. Occasionally shows extreme like happiest when happy and saddest when something goes wrong.

ᐳᐳᐳ

2. PARITA BUA

She is my crime partner at home and she is damn cute and funny. She helps me handle worst of family situations and relates to me like a friend . She motivates me for my career .

Being with her doesn't make me know of one generation gap I have with her...she is like my elder sister and we are duo while gossiping. Since childhood , my summer and winter vacations are pale and empty without her . And she gave me a nick name when I didn't know my name and no one calls me by that name after her marriage.

That's how she describes me :

"1. You are crazy about writing

2. You often don't sleep at nights.

3. You are a unique person.

4. You have very strong and different opinions about life ,nature and society .

5. You do tasks assigned to me in different jugadu ways.

6. You am kind of kamchor when it comes to household chores .

7. You am muhphat and outspoken.

8. You over react sometimes.

9. You want things to go by my way .

10. You take things too serious.

11 . You don't understand this concept of social rules .

12. You are dil ki saaf."

ᐳᐳᐳ

3. BITHA MOSI

The one I have argued with most (after mummy) . Mine and her opinions rarely match on any topic . Sometimes I find her dominating but she is also caring and helpful. We hardly can convince each other. She is broad minded and modern in her approach. She has chosen most of the dresses in my wardrobe and her fashion sense is great. As I grow up, I seek to develop an understanding with her.

That's how she describes me:

"She is very industrious deterministic girl .

She is down to earth.

She is unaware of capabilities she possess.

She has unique quality to control herself in adverse situation .

She is cooperative and supportive towards her friends "

She is a wonderful girl who believes in togetherness and if that doesn't happen suddenly becomes sad .

She has another side that is she trusts easily.

She has ups and downs in her life but while in down phase ,she takes more time to start again.

She is a gem of her friend circle .

She has a kind of naughty nature which makes her more strong to tackle her weakness."

ᐳᐳᐳ

4.SIDDHANT

He is my brother from another mother since the day we met at the end of our great 10th class . And the lots of memories we have related to adventurous 12th class which was tough one . We fight more than cats and dogs and sometimes it's gets too serious but it changes nothing between us. He has always supported me like my elder brother would had he existed!

That's how my school friend describes me:

"You are Helpful and caring .

You are revolutionary (always ready to speak against the odds)

You are a good counselor.

You are mentally strong.

You are a good teacher.

You are somewhat dumb.

You are completely different from today's genZ generation like away from drinking, smoking ,increasing body count and all this shit .

You are complete focused towards aims.

You are very careless.

You are very sensitive

You are little bit overthinker as well.

You are impudent (dheet)

You have sleepless nights"

ᐅᐅᐅ

5.SHUBHANGI

She is my college friend and have known me for less than a year but I vibe with her a lot. She really has a strong personality and charismatic persona. She is always ready for her friends ,takes stand for them and her motivating skills are just awesome. It didn't take much time for us to get close . She 'll always be an inalienable part of my college memories.

This is how she describes me:

"You are courageous and brave.

You are very strong mentally.

You keep smiling and is always cheerful.

You are disciplined and consistent.

You push yourself beyond limits.

You are honest.

You are caring.

You are empathetic.

You are understanding.
You are trustworthy.
You are supportive and loving."

ᑭᑭᑭ

6. DEVRAJ

My college companion who has helped get me away with last minute assignment submission ,practical tests and vivas. And he is the one whom look up to for pyqs and notes last night before exam. He is very gentle and understanding in his behavior. And kind of academic and career concerning discussions are always productive and enlightening.

This is how he describes me:

"You are really hardworking individual with lots of positivity in you.

You are very ambitions.

You never surrender easily or scumb to tough situations rather you fight back.

You always listen to positive which others give to you.

As a friend ,you are very supportive and caring.

As my bestie ,you never judge me and we share each and every problem small or big no matter .

You always take side of righteousness and weak.

You are very helpful to not only your friends but also to people who seek help from you .

You have a very fine sense of judgement .

You are a kind girl with a very pure heart."

ᑭᑭᑭ

7. Aayush

He is a great company in college and I have hit him during silly fights. Debates I have with him pertain to politics ,religion and society and most often...fight on who is more cute and whose height is perfect. He is a pure soul with a little bit rude face and words .

That's how he describes me :

"Tu achi hh
Tu helpful hh
Tu caring hh
Tera nature badhiya hh
Tu justice k liye ladti hh
Tu musibat m kaam aati hh"

ᐅᐅᐅ

8.RANA SINGH

The person I got into debate with on the very first day of college when I didn't know his name even and that debate is never ending but our friendship began this way . He is polite in his nature and joyful behaviour. He is patient and appreciative listener to my shyaris . His aura is energetic and too much active.

And this is how he describes me:

"She is the best Shayar (Urdu poet), I have ever heard .

She is an exceptionally good orater.

She is even very keen listener ,which makes her greater a person (even to people with ideological differences with her.

She is also very passionate and strong debater.

Her political and ideological differences with someone ,does not affect her friendship with that person, which in itself is very rare.

She believes that humanity is the greatest religion of the universe .

She is a very brave ,courageous and strong girl ,and an advocate of logical feminism (not Pseudo feminism)

Her personality has a very unique but philosophical depth.

She is a woman of her words and always abide by her values and moral beliefs.

She is also a stauch beleiver of the notion that ,Inner beauty of a person is what actually matters ,not the outer Bodily Beauty."

ᐅᐅᐅ